7-

D1225862

220,95
R89

The Biblical Philosophy Of History

By

ROUSAS J. RUSHDOONY

PRESBYTERIAN AND REFORMED PUBLISHING CO.
Phillipsburg, New Jersey
1977

Nyack College Library

Copyright 1969
The Craig Press
Rousas J. Rushdoony

Library of Congress Card Catalog No. 77-94222

Printed in the United States of America

275991

CONTENTS

THE AUTHOR

Rousas J. Rushdoony, editor of *Philosophical and Historical Studies* of the International Library of Philosophy and Theology, and of the University Series (*Historical Studies*), is an American writer and scholar. An ordained minister in the Orthodox Presbyterian Church, he has been a missionary among Paiute and Shoshone Indians as well as a pastor. Currently engaged in research, he lectures extensively. A contributor to many theological and philosophical journals, he is the author of *By What Standard?*, *Freud* and *Van Til* (Modern Thinkers Series), *Intellectual Schizophrenia, The Messianic Character of American Education, This Independent Republic, The Nature of the American System, The Myth of Over Population, Bread Upon the Waters, The Mythology of Science*, and *Foundations of the Social Order*.

I

THE BIBLICAL PHILOSOPHY OF HISTORY

The question, "What is history?," confronts the Christian scholar and student today with a great urgency. Accustomed as he is to believing that history is the story of what has happened in time, in terms of its major events and movements, the average man is little prepared to cope with the many new concepts of history which undergird modern historiography. In particular, Biblical scholars have indulged in the "search for the historical Jesus" with startling results, giving a report on a "demythologized" Jesus which bears no resemblance to the Jesus of the Bible. Church historians and secular historians likewise give a version of history as totally the product of impersonal natural forces, so that God and Christ become not only abstracted from past history but very remote to the present.

What is history? Out of the millions of events and persons of the past, how are certain events selected as significant? Is the Battle of Stalingrad in 1942–1943 as important as or more important than the Battle of Avarair in 451? On what ground do we stress the one and neglect the other? And when is an event "history"?

The problem can best be recognized by analyzing some remarks of an important contemporary theologian, an Episcopalian layman who, since 1961, has been Associate Professor of Bible and Religion at Emory University, Atlanta, Georgia. Thomas J. Altizer holds that the "first requirement" of any intellectual inquiry which will break the

1

impasse of modern thought "is a forthright confession of the death of the God of Christendom, a full acknowledgement that the era of Christian civilization has come to an end, with the result that all cognitive meaning and all moral values that were once historically associated with the Christian God have collapsed." This death of God means not only that we recognize that the historic faith was mythical but that we also recognize it to be dead as an historical influence: "God has died in *our* time, in *our* history, in *our* existence."[1] This means that history has a totally new meaning because God is dead. "This meaning of 'historical' is intimately related to the modern idea of 'historicity': for, in this perspective, 'historicity' means a total immersion in historical time, an immersion that is totally isolated from any meaning or reality that might lie beyond it."[2] Modern man's life is existential; this means "an absolute autonomy which finally encloses him within the concrete moment itself."[3] In terms of this faith, history can have no transcendental meaning. The life of Jesus must be read in exclusively naturalistic terms; nothing can be "historical" if it represents a supernatural power, act, or influence. Jesus is accordingly "demythologized," and this "Jesus of history" bears no resemblance to the Jesus of Scripture, who is God incarnate and the Messiah of prophecy. "Total immersion in historical time" means that any and every event "is totally isolated from any meaning or reality that might lie beyond it." Such a faith clearly excludes the Biblical God from *all* history, which must be read in terms of the purely naturalistic and immanent forces of the present. This means also that the basic drives of history are natural and hence primarily impersonal, since the vast

[1] Thomas J. J. Altizer: *Mircea Eliade and the Dialectic of the Sacred*, p. 13. Philadelphia: Westminster Press, 1963.

[2] *Ibid.*, p. 23.

[3] *Ibid.*, p. 26.

2

reservoir of being is basically an impersonal and totally natural ocean of blind movement and energy. History therefore is both "demythologized" of the sacred and also depersonalized.

The Biblical philosophy of history is clearly and irrevocably at odds with the modern faith. Basic to the Biblical philosophy is the doctrine of creation. This doctrine has far-reaching implications for history. *First*, the doctrine of creation asserts that the universe, time, history, man, and all things are the handiwork of a sovereign, omnipotent, omniscient, and triune God. *Second*, this means that the meaning of history is to be understood primarily and essentially in terms of that God. Time and history are created by God and therefore are determined and governed by God. The ground of history, therefore, is not in time, not in a total immersion in the moment, but in eternity. *Third*, creation is described by all of Scripture as a creative *act* of God, in six days, and thus it must be understood as *act, not process*. Every attempt to read process into the creation account, to turn the days into ages and make room for "scientific" interpretations, is a surrender to process philosophies and an abandonment of the sovereignty of God. It ascribes powers to a natural process and weakens the determinative power of the creative act. The Biblical account is explicit in its description: we are told of a series of perfect and final acts. We are not given a report on processes. The creative acts are not only perfect and final: they are totally supernatural. This is their offense. To give man an "historical" doctrine of creation, in the modern sense of that term, it is necessary to supplant the creative act with a creative process, so that the initiative is at the very least placed within history if not made totally a product of history. Such theologians are philosophical immersionists; the only God they can tolerate is on who is immersed in history, one who is Himself a product of natural process

3

and is working together with man to conquer time and history. God and man are thus partners and co-workers in the war against brute factuality. According to Justin Wroe Nixon, "To those, whose sentiments are voiced by Walter Rauschenbusch, God is the dynamic of progress, the central reality of a forward-moving life." [4] In this perspective, God is not the Creator; instead, He is another creature, although a greater one, who is leading man in the battle against the forces of chaos. He has not created time and history but rather appears in time and history to give meaning to it by conquering it and reshaping it to His hopes. As a result, God is the spearhead of a revolution in time and history against the chaos and meaninglessness of time and history.

There is little question that the changes which seem imminent in our conception of the functions of God will be disturbing. But they are not lacking in promise. Under their influence we shall think of God as the atmosphere and the assumption of the highest life. He furnishes its setting. He is to be found in the realm of appreciation rather than of manipulation. Because he is an Order he is the vision of unrealized achievement in every realm and because He is a Person He is yet our unfailing resource in defeat. He meets every man on the level of his own need and yet He draws us all into the corporate spiritual union of all mankind. The experience of God will probably always come to us as a medicine, a remedy for emergencies, but it will seem more and more like the glow of health and joy and the unforgettable vision which one brings back from a walk over the hills. God is the end of life, an end which is beyond life but which alone brings us to the fullest realization of ourselves in life. Because He is the lure and the imperative in the Best that we know He is indeed "the substance of all revolutions." [5]

[4] Justin Wroe Nixon: *An Emerging Christian Faith*, p. 127. New York: Harper, 1930.

[5] *Ibid.*, p. 160.

The God of the Bible is the Creator of all things; man is in rebellion against God and His law, and the basic problem of man is sin. History is the battle of Christ versus antichrist, and man's basic need is redemption through the blood of Jesus Christ and then life in Christ and under God's law, now no longer a bill of indictment against man but a charter for life. For this perspective presented by Nixon, man's basic problem is not sin against God but the need to realize his potentialities in history by conquering nature and giving it meaning, by a war against chaos. But his faith is itself an assertion of chaos, in that revolution is essential to it, and God is "the substance of all revolutions." There is no need for reconciliation to this God; instead, He is our head revolutionist in uniting all mankind in gaining their goal, revolution. Not a new man in Jesus Christ, but a new order, a grand revolution against a hostile universe, led by the First Revolutionist, God, is the hope of this faith. The universe is not the creation of this God but His enemy, territory to be conquered with man's help. God Himself is finite, a creature of the universe who is spearheading revolution against it, striving together with man to attain His ideals. God is thus the great process of revolution. The Jesus of this faith is an unreservedly human being like ourselves. It can be said, however, that "God was in Christ" in that the vision of "the Best" and all God's hopes for His great revolution found expression in Jesus. The potentialities of man and of history come into focus in Jesus.[6] This is the *best* God and Christ that process philosophy can give us, and this is clearly a Christ who cannot save but can only lead and inspire man.

Fourth, the Biblical doctrine of creation not only asserts that creation is the creative act of God but, because it is totally His creative act, creation is totally under His government. Another word for this total government is pre-

[6] *Ibid.*, p. 201.

5

destination. Because our age is so thoroughly humanistic, it is in rebellion against predestination, which is simply the assertion of God's sovereignty, government, and control. Humanism insists that man must be in control, and socialism and communism, as well as scientific planning, psychological controls, and other attempts of man to control man and nature, are simply assertions of predestination by man. The only alternative to the doctrine of predestination is the assertion of the reign of total chance, of meaninglessness and brute factuality. The real issue is what kind of predestination we shall have, predestination by God or predestination by man? Shall we accept God's eternal decree, His total planning, or will we submit to man's total planning, man's dream of playing god and planner over all creation? According to the Biblical faith, God alone is God, God alone is the first cause. This means that God alone has absolute freedom and power. Man's freedom is the liberty of a second cause; it is genuine liberty, but it is limited because man is a creature, and it is subordinate to the total creation and determination of all things by the triune God. Whenever and wherever the doctrine of creation is denied or weakened, to that extent the sovereignty of God and His eternal decree are denied or weakened, and sovereignty and predestinating power are transferred into the hands of man. Man, as the high point of process and evolution, becomes also the high point of history and of the power of prediction and predestination.

When men began to depart from Biblical faith, they turned to ancient classical thought with its pagan faith in natural law. The doctrine of natural law asserts the presence in nature of inherent laws which govern reality, so that law is transferred from God to nature. Law is no longer *over* creation but *within* process. The concept of natural law, confused by Christians with God's providence in nature and the total subservience of all nature to God's decree and law, made great inroads into Christian thinking and became the mainspring of Enlightenment faith in its rejection of the God of Scripture. Classical liberalism is based on this Enlightenment faith, as is modern libertarianism and conservatism. Nature has, inherent within itself, its own processes and laws which govern reality. Hence, man's attitude is one of *laissez-faire*; there must be no interference with nature's laws and controls. Planning was thus transferred from God to nature. Darwinism destroyed this faith in nature. The process of nature was now portrayed, not as a perfect working of law, but as a blind, unconscious energy working profligately to express itself. In the struggle for survival, the fittest survive by virtue of their own adaptations, not because of natural law. Nature produces many "mistakes" which fail to survive and become extinct species and fossils. The destiny of the universe is extinction as its energy runs down.

All of this served to shatter the older faith in nature. Nature as the agency of predestination was gone. It became increasingly evident to naturalistic thinkers that man must control his own evolution and also control the evolution of plant and animal life. Moreover, man must create and control his own social order, so that total statism, total socialism, is "scientific socialism," that is, socialism which recognizes that man cannot exist without predestination and therefore provides for the control of process, for total planning and predestination, by the elite men. Centuries ago, Plato came to a similar conclusion and charted the course for total tyranny in his infamous *Republic*. The same planning and control by man, predestination by man, is again a major force in history. Socialism, statist education, mental health programs, social security, and a variety of other statist programs provide the framework for man's growing attempt to claim the power of predestination for himself. Man seeks, in short, to become

7

his own savior and god.

Fifth, the source of energy and power is radically different in the Biblical faith than in the humanistic creed. For the orthodox Christian, who grounds his philosophy of history on the doctrine of creation, the mainspring of history is God. Time rests on the foundation of eternity, on the eternal decree of God. Time and history therefore have meaning because they were created in terms of God's perfect and totally comprehensive plan. Every blade of grass, every sparrow's fall, the very hairs of our head, all are comprehended and governed by God's eternal decree, and all have meaning in terms of it. The humanist faces a meaningless world in which he must strive to create and establish meaning. The Christian accepts a world which is totally meaningful and in which *every* event moves in terms of God's predestined purpose, and, when man accepts God as his Lord and Christ as his Savior, *every* event works together for good to him because he is now in harmony with that meaning and destiny (Rom. 8:28). Man therefore does not create meaning; instead, having rebelled against God's meaning, having striven to be as God and himself the source of meaning and definition (Gen. 3:5), man now submits to God's meaning and finds his life therein. For the humanist, the dynamics of history are in titanic man, as he imposes his will and idea on the world. For the orthodox Christian, the dynamics of history are in God the Creator, and man accepts those dynamics and rejoices in the blessings thereof when man accepts Christ as Savior and then follows the leadings of the sanctifying Holy Spirit. For him, the Bible is the authoritative, inspired and infallible word of the triune God.

Sixth, the Biblical philosophy of history is grounded not only on the doctrine of creation but on the doctrine of the infallible Scripture. A God who is struggling together with man against the darkness of a universe of brute factuality,

8

is a God who is struggling to realize Himself. He cannot therefore speak predictively but only hopefully, because He is not in total control. Again, because He has not fully realized Himself, He is not fully self-conscious, so that His word lacks perspicuity and lucidity; it cannot be infallible, because He is neither perfect, omnipotent, nor sovereign. It can merely be an inspiring exhortation from another and leading "freedom fighter." But the orthodox doctrine holds to the infallible word because it recognizes that God created all things, governs all things, and knows all things, and "known unto God are all his works, from the beginning of the world" (Acts 15:18). A perfect, omnipotent and totally self-conscious God can *only* speak infallibly: His word is *inescapably* an infallible word. A limited God can no more speak infallibly than he can predestine. He is not in full control of either the universe or himself.

The hostility of modernists and atheists to the doctrine of infallibility as applied to Scripture rests on the same foundation as their hostility to predestination. Man claims increasingly the right to total planning, and man claims increasingly, as he refines his scientific method, the power to speak authoritatively in a creative sense.

Octavius Brooks Frothingham (1822–1895), Unitarian and humanist, in his important work, *The Religion of Humanity*, stated the totally immanent doctrine of infallibility succinctly:

> The interior spirit of any age is the spirit of God; and no faith can be living that has that spirit against it; no Church can be strong except in that alliance. The life of the time appoints the creed of the time and modifies the establishment of the time.[7]

The implications of this position are far-reaching. First,

[7] O. B. Frothingham: *The Religion of Humanity*, p. 7f. New York: G. P. Putnam's Sons, 1875. Third Edition. For Frothingham, humanity is God.

because there is no truth beyond man, "the interior spirit of any age" is made infallible and inspired. This is the essence of modernism, the demand that the church submit to the spirit and science of the age as authoritative, because there can be no truth, life, or faith apart from it or beyond it. If historicity is "total immersion in historical time, an immersion that is totally isolated from any meaning or reality that might lie beyond it," as Altizer stated, then to speak with inspiration and with infallibility is to express completely and without reservation that "interior spirit of any age" we live in, the infallibility Frothingham called for. The existentialist today gives the best expression of this concept. Second, since this truth, an infallible truth, is without any transcendental reference, it is a truth which changes from age to age; as Frothingham said, "The life of the times appoints the creed of the times." Every age has its new spirit, its new truth, and its new infallible word. And since man cannot transcend himself or his age, and has no transcendental truth, man's organized spirit, the state, becomes the infallible word over man. The reign of the great harlot state, Babylon, is thus enthroned by humanism with infallibility and sovereignty. When man denies the infallible word of God he very quickly faces the infallible State of man. Unless man lives with and in Christ in terms of "*every* word that proceedeth out of the mouth of God" (Matt. 4:4), he cannot escape the historical determinism of an infallible state, whether the Marxist version or another. Thus man, in seeking to wrest control of history from the hand of God, has made himself instead the prisoner of history, and, moreover, a prisoner without hope.

Seventh, the Biblical philosophy of history means that time does not come out of a primeval past but from eternity. The origin of time is not in chaos but in eternity. Evolutionary time emerges out of the past, gropes its way blindly into the present, and moves sightlessly into an unknown

10

future. The movement of time is thus from the past to the present into the future. The movement of time, according to the Bible, is from eternity, since it is created by God and moves out of and in terms of His eternal decree. Because time moves in terms of the eternal decree, when its function is finished there shall be time no more (Rev. 10:6). Because time is predestined, and because its beginning and end are already established, time does not develop in evolutionary fashion from past to present to future. Instead, it unfolds from future to present to past. In Wood's words, "The future is the source, it is the reservoir of time which some day will be present, and then past." [8] Better stated, eternity is the source; time is predestined, and therefore it moves from the future to the present to the past. "The future is logically first, but not chronologically." [9]

The Past issues, it proceeds, from the Future, through the Present.

The Present therefore comes out from the invisible Future. The Present perpetually and ever-newly embodies the Future in visible, audible, livable form; and returns again into invisible Time in the Past.

The Past acts invisibly. It continually influences us with regard to the Present. It casts light upon the Present. That is its great function. It helps us to live in the Present which we know, and with reference to the Future which we expect to see.[10]

For evolutionary time, the past is determinative. The source of time and of being is in primeval chaos, and it is primeval chaos, the great and creative Past, which has been hence determinative heretofore, and it is this time and being born of chaos that man now seeks to control and determine. The

[8] Nathan R. Wood: *The Secret of the Universe*, p. 44. Grand Rapids: Eerdmans, 1936, 1955.

[9] *Ibid.*, p. 45.

[10] *Ibid.*, p. 45.

11

source of Biblical time is eternity; flowing from an eternal decree and a determined end to a determined past, it is experienced by man chronologically from past to present to future. In faith, man recognizes that God "hath determined the times before appointed" (Acts 17:26), and he can declare in faith, "My times are in thy hand" (Psalm 31:15). The evolutionists seeks to determine the future as a predestinating god, but he is also inescapably bound to a primeval chaos as less than man. He understands himself, to use Cornelius Van Til's phrase, in terms of a psychology of primitivism which is "integration into the void." His psychology wipes out "the borderline that separated man from the beast, and the beast from the inorganic world, thus reducing man to a focus of action and interaction in the sea of an ultimate irrationalism." [11] This concept takes away responsibility from man, for "Man cannot be responsible to the void." Man "frees" himself from God's predestination only by positing instead an "ultimate irrationalism" and man becomes as a result free for irresponsibility. "Man is responsible in the whole of his personality but only if he is the creature of God. Man *before God* is the only alternative to man *in the void*." [12]

An *eighth* implication of the doctrine of creation for the Biblical philosophy of history has reference to the nature of man. If nature generated man, then man is wholly passive in relationship to nature but active in relationship to any God that exists. But if God created man, man is wholly passive in relationship to God, but he is active in relationship to nature as God's image-bearer. If man is the creature of nature, then, however much he may hope to dominate and control nature, he is still basically its creature, conditioned by nature and subordinate to it. It is significant that, despite the dreams of total control,

[11] Cornelius Van Til: *Psychology of Religion*, p. 57. Syllabus, 1935.
[12] *Ibid.*, p. 62.

the psychologies formulated by non-Christian man are *passive* psychologies. Man is made a product of his heredity and environment. His mind is passive and malleable. The mind of man has been compared to a blank sheet of white paper, and his nature seen as neutral. This neutral, bland man receives sense impressions from the world and responds to them and is conditioned by them. The explicit faith of non-Christian psychology in the power of conditioned reflexes is grounded in this passive psychology; the concept of the predestination of man and his society by the elite rests on this passivist psychology of man. *Conditioning rather than education* becomes the function of the statist school.[13] There is a grim irony in this situation: the more the scientific state develops as a god, the more it rests on the premise that man is passive and can be subjected to total conditioning. Man, in brief, is made more and more subject to nature, more and more passive in relationship to nature, while, in the "person" of the corporate state, he wages unremitting and active warfare against God and claims the prerogatives of God.

The orthodox Christian must assert, however, that, because God created man, this statist dream is a myth: it cannot be realized. Man is created in the image of God, and man is either a covenant-keeper or a covenant-breaker. As a covenant-breaker, man is in bondage to sin and to death; having no peace with God because of his sin, man has no peace with his fellow men and no peace with himself. He is in slavery to the state, not because he is by nature passive in relationship to his environment, but because he is in sin and is reaping the wages of sin. The destiny of covenant-keeping man is to be God's vicegerent in Christ, to be God's priest, prophet, and king over creation, to rule, interpret, understand, and dedicate the world in Christ

[13] See R. J. Rushdoony: *The Messianic Character of American Education.* Nutley, New Jersey: The Craig Press, 1963.

unto God the Father. Man is not passive in his relationship to nature; rather, nature is passive in relationship to man. Nature was passive in receiving the consequences of man's fall, and nature is passive today as man's sin lays nature waste. Nature will be passive again in receiving her sabbath rests from man's hands, and it will finally share passively in man's glorification (Rom. 8:19-22). Man is passive in relationship to God, and man's sin and ruin are due to his attempts to free himself from this passivity and to become independent and autonomously active and creative. The non-Christian doctrine places man *under nature* and seeks to place him *over God*; the Biblical doctrine places man *under God*, and *over nature* in Him. Thus, the consequence of *every* philosophy of history which denies the God of Scripture, His infallible word and His creative act, is to open the way for the terror of man under nature and under the divine and messianic state.

A *ninth* implication of the doctrine of creation and of the ontological trinity for the philosophy of history is that all factuality is, as Van Til has repeatedly pointed out, made personal, because it is the handiwork of the personal and triune God, and it derives its meaning from His personal, creative act and eternal decree. The factuality of non-Christian philosophy is impersonal factuality at best and basically meaningless brute factuality. Thus, the best interpretation of reality which evolutionary philosophies of history can give man reduces history to sub-personal and sub-human forces. For the Darwinist, history is the product of impersonal biological forces; for the Marxist, the forces are economic, for the Freudian, psychological and unconscious. Not only is the meaning of history de-personalized, but man is de-personalized as well. Man begins by asserting the supremacy of his autonomous mind and reason and ends in total irrationalism. As Van Til has often stated, the fate of rationalism is total irrationalism, and irrationalism rests on rationalism. When man makes himself and his reason god over creation, he thereupon destroys all meaning in creation and leaves himself a chained and gibbering baboon, sitting in terror on a wired electric chair in the midst of a vast universe of nothingness.

Every non-biblical philosophy of history ends by destroying both man and history. It begins by striving to give a better meaning to history than the one eternity provides, and it ends by robbing history of any human meaning and man of his manhood. In taking counsel against God and His decree, man effectually hurts only himself, not God. In rebelling against the kingship of Christ over history and in seeking to establish his own autonomous kingship, man reduces himself to the status of a slave.

A century ago, a popular American preacher, in addressing the cultured despisers of Christ, who were as yet in his day morally and culturally Christianized, declared:

But O, ye godless men of reason, of integrity in your relations to your fellow men; ye godless women of culture, of influence, of social recognition, *be warned by this truth*. Howsoever refined, howsoever influential ye may be, still, without Christ you are a condemned rebel against Almighty God. You stand defying this power which is above. Your heart says, even if your lips are silent, "I will not have this man to rule over me." The Spirit of God holds forth to each one of you either the sceptre of His grace, or the rod of His wrath. Every reasonable subject must choose. Thou canst never dethrone Jesus Christ. Thou canst never cast Him out of the universe. Thou canst submit to Him and that is all that thou canst do. Thou mayest submit to Him now, and receive all the comforts of His reign, or thou mayest reject Him; but if the latter, there shall certainly come a time when thou shalt gnash thy teeth in hopelessness and despair because thou wouldest have none of His rule and reign.

Dear brother, dear hearer, be persuaded that there is another King, one Jesus. Yield thy life to Him. Enter into

15

His service. Begin to be loyal. Cease to be a rebel. Wise is he who submits to the rule of this King.[14]

In the words of the psalmist, "Kiss the Son, lest he be angry, and ye perish from the way, when his wrath is kindled but a little. Blessed are all they that put their trust in him" (Psalm 2:12).

To accept this Biblical philosophy means to accept the responsibility of the creation mandate. Man must exercise dominion in the name of God, and in knowledge, righteousness, and holiness. Education must be Christian, because all non-Christian education is committed to beliefs which are either implicitly or explicitly at war with the Christian faith. Christian education must also be philosophically informed and epistemologically self-conscious: it cannot be Christian unless it re-thinks every area of study in terms of a consistent and systematic Biblical faith.

The world, moreover, cannot be surrendered to Satan. It is God's world and must be brought under God's law, politically, economically, and in every other way possible.

The Enlightenment, by its savage and long-standing attack on Biblical faith, has brought about a long retreat of Christianity from a full-orbed faith to a kind of last-ditch battle centering around the doctrines of salvation and of the infallible Scripture. The time has come for a full-scale offensive, and it has indeed begun, to bring every area of thought into captivity to Christ, to establish the whole counsel of God and every implication of His infallible word.

For the orthodox Christian, history is determined by eternity, and "the eternal does not exist for us as a principal but as a person, and that as an absolute person." Moreover, "For us God's being is ultimate, while created

[14] *The People's Pulpit: Containing Sermons by Stephen H. Tyng, Jr. D.D.*, Vol. VI, p. 249 f. New York: The People's Pulpit Company, 1878.

being is, in the nature of the case, derivative." [15] The very meaning and glory of history is its derivative nature. Humanistic history is a shaking and frail ladder, resting on no foundation and reaching out into nothingness, whereas history under God rests in total meaning and purpose and gives man a glorious inheritance and destiny, for

> God from all eternity did by the most wise and holy counsel of his own will freely and unchangeably ordain whatsoever comes to pass: yet so as thereby neither is God the author of sin, nor is violence offered to the will of creatures, nor is the liberty or contingency of second causes taken away, but rather established. [16]

[15] Cornelius Van Til: *The Defense of the Faith*, p. 46. Philadelphia: Presbyterian and Reformed Publishing Company, 1955.
[16] The Westminster Confession of Faith, Chapter III, 1.

II

THE DIMENSION OF VICTORY

More than a few men have seen history as meaningless frustration. Poetry giving vent to this mood has repeatedly met with a response from many men who respond to Macbeth's bitter words:

> To-morrow, and to-morrow, and to-morrow,
> Creeps in this petty pace from day to day,
> To the last syllable of recorded time;
> And all our yesterdays have lighted fools
> The way to dusty death. Out, out, brief candle!
> Life's but a walking shadow; a poor player,
> That struts and frets his hour upon the stage,
> And then is heard no more: it is a tale
> Told by an idiot, full of sound and fury,
> Signifying nothing.
> (*Macbeth*, Act V, Scene v.)

In this perspective, man's destiny is death and frustration, and life's only meaning is the grim mockery of witches. Matthew Arnold in *Dover Beach*, concluded that

> . . . . the world, which seems
> To lie before us like a land of dreams,
> So various, so beautiful, so new,
> Hath really neither joy, nor love, nor light,
> Nor certitude, nor peace, nor help for pain;
> And we are here as on a darkling plain
> Swept with confused alarms of struggle and flight
> Where ignorant armies clash by night.

T. S. Eliot stated it more bluntly in *The Hollow Men*:

> This is the way the world ends
> Not with a bang but a whimper.

In such a perspective, history not only lacks victory: it also lacks meaning. But man cannot live without meaning. Nothing is more destructive of man than meaningless activity and living. Accordingly, those who have agreed that life and history are meaningless either must in effect commit suicide, physically or spiritually, or else attempt to force a meaning and a victory onto history.

Man's chosen instrument in this attempt to force purpose and victory onto history is *science*. Science is seen as control and prediction, and by means of science, man must control history and make it totally predictable. History must be reduced to a province of science; history must become a laboratory in which man is experimented on for the purpose of making a meaningless history purposeful. The purpose is to be derived from the scientific thought of the sociological planners. In this perspective, history is a *social science*, and the meaning of history as social science is simply that society and societal relations are a province of science and derive their meaning and content from scientific control and prediction.

In this perspective, God has no part in history; man makes history. It is not God's creation, for God is a mythical projection of man's mind. History as a social science is thus radically opposed to the Biblical faith that history is God's handiwork. The history textbooks of our day, as well as most historical research, approach history as a social science; as a result, they are implicitly anti-Christian, and dependence upon them lays down an unconscious and deep foundation of anti-Christian presuppositions.

History as man's scientific creation means history totally controlled by the scientific elite. Since God's predestination is ruled out, man's predestination or total planning must take its place. History, which for orthodox Christianity is closely linked to theology, now becomes an associate of sociology. The purpose of history ceases to be understanding; it becomes an instrument of control. "The children of the state" are given indoctrination in this re-interpreted history in order to make them amenable to the controls of today and tomorrow, to the purposes of the socialist state. On the other hand, the children of God are taught that history has as its mainstream the Messianic purpose of Jesus Christ. In Rendall's words, "it *is* the main tide of history: all others are tributary. The Messianic purpose holds together the entire fabric of history, integrating all things in Christ." [1]

Non-Christian religions lack this Messianic purpose. The pagan nature-mythologies saw history as "endlessly-recurring cycles of events."

> These mythical heroes and goddesses symbolized processes of nature, and in particular the natural cycles of the seasons. Transferred as a thought-form to collective human experience they also express mythologically the rise and decline of successive generations as the ultimate norm of human history. So expressed, history moves onward by a sort of natural necessity in an endless chain of perpetually-repeated events, having no fixed point of beginning, and leading up to no conclusive ending.[2]

In the pagan perspective, man is a creature of nature, not of God, and man is therefore to be understood in terms of nature. But in the Biblical perspective, man is God's creation, directly related to God, and set over the world of nature rather than under it. Man cannot be reduced to a natural process, nor his history to a social science.

[1] Robert Rendall: *History, Prophecy and God*, p. 62. London: Paternoster Press, 1954.
[2] *Ibid.*, p. 37. Cf. Herbert Butterfield: *Christianity and History*, p. 1ff. New York: Scribner's, 1950. Butterfield's position, however, is not Biblical and lacks any eternal decree; cf. pp. 93-112.

History as a social science is concerned with escaping the defeat echoed by the poets. Instead of being "a tale told by an idiot, full of sound and fury, signifying nothing," life and history as a social science, are to be made into a victory by means of total control and prediction. This means socialism, scientific socialism, and the purpose of socialism is to give a dimension of victory to history. An important factor in its success is the fact that Christian eschatology has increasingly surrendered the dimension of victory and emphasized the dimension of tribulation as the essence of the future.

But this is scarcely the Biblical view, by no means the temper of Scripture nor of Biblical theologians in the great ages of the faith. St. Paul, faced with the trials of the saints, declared, "What shall we then say to these things? If God be for us, who can be against us?" (Rom. 8:31). The sovereignty of God over history is emphatically the Biblical view. God predestines, creates, and totally governs all history.

Very early in his struggle with Rome, Martin Luther observed, "God alone is in this business; we are seized so that I see we are acted upon rather than act." [3] Luther thus saw history as the work of God. He stood in Biblical tradition as upheld by Augustine and very soon by Calvin also. This theocentric perspective concerning history separates him from modern historiography. Moreover, as Headley has observed,

This difference is not limited to the problem of causation but appears in its two immediate implications: that every action derived from God gives unity and meaning to history, and, secondly, because man is the instrument of God one is denied the luxury of being a spectator. Man is constantly being acted upon and serves as a cooperator in this action. This unbroken activity of God pushes man

[3] Cited in John M. Headley: *Luther's View of Church History*, p. 1. New Haven: Yale University Press, 1963.

into an unbroken cooperation in history. In such a situation there can be no dead history and no flight from history.[4]

It was this triumphant faith which Luther expressed in his hymn, "A Mighty Fortress Is Our God":

> And though this world, with devils filled,
> Should threaten to undo us,
> We will not fear, for God hath willed
> His truth to triumph through us.

It was this strong sense of victory which enabled the early church to withstand fearful persecution and to triumph. This dimension of victory was basic also to the Reformation and to the American Puritans. Today, however, vast segments of the church have joined the enemy and preach the gospel according to Caesar, and too often those who profess the faith in Christ think in terms of defeat and the retreat of the church before evil rather than a decree and mandate of victory. The retreat of the Christian Church is first of all a retreat from faith. History has been surrendered to the devil because the faith has been either surrendered or compromised.

What are some of the basic premises of a Biblical philosophy of history? Before we can restore the dimension of victory, we must restore the faith that assures victory.

First of all, in the Biblical perspective, history is the handiwork of God because the whole universe is His creation. History cannot be downgraded or dismissed as illusion. Non-Christian philosophies inevitably find time and history a problem. Monism reduces all being to one; it emphasizes the unity and oneness of being, and it therefore downgrades and minimizes the meaning of particularity, of individuals, and of history, which is the story of the struggles of particulars rather than a demonstration

[4] *Ibid.*, p. 2.

of the unity of being. Monism, moreover, tends steadily to minimize the world of matter; in Indian thought, it is the world of Maya, of illusion. Maya is "the 'veil' covering reality, the experience of manifoldness when only the One is real." [5] Western monism, not as far developed as Eastern, has not yet reduced the world of particulars to Maya, but is well on its way. The state is the reality, and the individual is increasingly only "real" as a member of the state. As Eby and Arrowood summarized Dewey's perspective, "An individual cannot be regarded, according to Dr. Dewey, as a being apart from society." [6] Our society and world are becoming increasingly monistic, and monism means the triumph of the one, of the state, or the unity of being, but this requires the defeat and submersion of the many, of the individual, and of the historical process. Marxist monism thus sees victory as the end of history and the beginning of post-historical man, although Marxism is in origin dialectical.

Dualism offers no better hope of victory. For dualism, the world is in perpetual tension or conflict between two hostile forces, the good god and the evil god, between light and dark, spirit and matter, the noumenal and the phenomenal, and man is thus assured of continuous conflict without victory, plus a downgrading of the material world and of history. Dualism has been a continuing undercurrent in Western thought, but there has also been a continuing revolt against the implications of dualism and of monism as well.

The attempt to avoid these twin evils of dualism and monism is dialecticism. Dialectical philosophy seeks to avoid these two evils, dualism and monism, and it affirms two

[5] Kurt F. Leidecker, "Maya," in Dagobert D. Runes: *Dictionary of Philosophy*, p. 191. New York: Philosophical Library, 1960.
[6] C. F. Arrowood and F. Eby: *The Development of Modern Education, In Theory, Organization and Practice*, p. 869. New York: Prentice-Hall, 1947.

apparently irreconcilable concepts without resolving their tension. Dialectical thought as a result breaks down, as one aspect triumphs over the other and either falls into monism, dualism, or atomism.

In the Biblical perspective, the doctrine of the Trinity gives equal ultimacy to the one and the many, so that the hopeless alternatives of dualism and monism are both avoided. History is neither illusion nor frustration, but the outworking of God's eternal decree. Biblical doctrine is not formulated in abstraction as in monistic religions. It is revealed in history and, in writing, woven into the context of the history of God's covenant with man. The Old Testament is a long record of such history, and the New Testament also. The doctrines expounded in the Epistles are not stated in abstraction but in terms of the realities of heresies, church problems, the revelation of Jesus Christ, and the destiny of God's elect people. History is important precisely because it is totally meaningful because of God's eternal decree and act of creation. The Council of Jerusalem declared, "Known unto God are all his works from the beginning of the world" (Acts 15:18). History is in the hands neither of chaos or of the social scientist but in the hands of the sovereign and triune God. Any adherence to chance, or to monism and dualism, and dialecticism as well, reduces history to frustration and gives no hope except the hopelessly totalitarian answer of social science. The eternal decree of the triune God alone assures meaning and victory for life and history.

A *second* aspect of the faith which assures victory is a sound doctrine of the resurrection. From more than a few philosophical and religious perspectives, the resurrection is foolishness. The goal of being and of man is seen as a transcending of the material for the spiritual. Both monism and dualism share this perspective. The realm of spirit is the higher realm, the true and good realm, whereas matter

24

represents a lower world, evil, and an aspect of life which man must overcome and transcend. Such a view is not Biblical. Both man's body and soul were created wholly good by God, and both alike are fallen and in need of the redemptive work of Jesus Christ. It is not the spirit which is good as against matter as evil, but man who is totally depraved by his fall into sin and totally saved by the work of Jesus Christ.

The purpose of Biblical history is to trace the victory of Jesus Christ. *That victory is not merely spiritual; it is also historical.* Creation, man, and man's body, all move in terms of a glorious destiny for which the whole creation groans and travails as it awaits the fulness of that glorious liberty of the sons of God (Rom. 8:18-23). The victory is historical and eschatalogical, and it is not the rejection of creation but its fulfilment.

This victory was set forth in the resurrection of Jesus Christ, Who destroyed the power of sin and death and emerged victorious from the grave. As St. Paul emphasized in I Corinthians 15, this victory is the victory of all believers. Christ is the firstfruit, the beginning, the alpha and omega of the life of the saints. Had Christ merely arisen as a spirit from the grave, it would have signified His lordship over the world of spirit but His surrender of matter and history. But by His physical resurrection, by His rising again in the same body with which He was crucified, He set forth His lordship over creation and over history. The world of history will see Christ's triumph and the triumph of His saints, His church, and His kingdom. History will not end in tribulation and disaster: it will see the triumph of the people of God and the manifestation of Christian order from pole to pole before Christ comes again. The doctrine of the resurrection is thus a cornerstone of the Biblical dimension of victory.

The doctrine of the resurrection, however, does not last

25

long in any church or philosophy which surrenders or compromises the doctrine of creation. Creationism asserts that the world is the creative act of the triune God, Who made it wholly good. Sin is a perversion of man and a deformation of creation. The goal of the Messianic purpose of history is the "restitution of all things" (Acts 3:21), their fulfilment in Jesus Christ, first in time and then in eternity. The words of Schilder beautifully sum up this faith:

> The supper of the marriage of the Lamb, the feast of all the household of God, with Christ, before God, assures us that heaven does not turn its back upon *history*. The future glory of Christ will ever be seen as a result of His humiliation. Paul tells us, in Philippians 2, that Christ was exalted because of the humiliation to which he had subjected Himself, thus closely linking Christ's life upon earth with His life in heaven. In calling the Great Supper "The Supper of the *Lamb*" heaven acknowledges the importance of history. The Lamb stands there as slain. That is to say, heaven never, throughout all eternity, abstracts Christ's exaltation (His standing) from His humiliation (His being slain). To the Lamb who wrought salvation for us by His blood will be given honor through all eternity. In that which is seen and said at the Great Supper, justice is done through all eternity to the fullness of God's work in history.

> In the Great Supper the meaning of history becomes clear. . . .

The historical reality of Christ's death and resurrection, then, is held in remembrance eternally in heaven. History is thus shown to be wholly governed by the sovereignty of God. And we reject wholly the conception of Dante, who, in his poem, refers to the mythological river Lethe. Of this mythological river of the underworld the dead must drink in order to forget the past. In his ascent through the heavenly spheres to the sun, the poet stops beside this river to rid himself of the oppressive memory of sin—by which he virtually meant that which is temporal, the relative, the historical. The poet would forget earth and all its aspects of time and space, for the higher the soul soars the more foolish and insignificant the earth and all things earthly become. And only after crossing the river is Dante privileged to meet that strange procession including a triumphal chariot escorted by the four-and-twenty elders and the four living creatures and the winged creatures, and surrounded by female figures who symbolize the church triumphant. And only after bathing once again in Lethe may Dante join the festal procession.

Such mythical ideas are riddled with neoplatonism. . . . When the doors of heaven open, all historical life upon earth loses its worth, they say. History no longer has meaning. But, contrary to this rejection of history, the Bible utters those beautiful words "the marriage supper of the Lamb." Those who have been called to this supper have not been bathed in Lethe; on the contrary, they commemorate *the center of history*; they receive a perspective of history from its beginning to its end.[7]

There is thus a dimension of victory in history, Jesus Christ. The alternative plan of victory is social science, and history as a social science. This means the totalitarian socialist state, the world of *1984*. For the Christian this is rather the dimension of hell, not of victory; for the believer, "this is the victory that overcometh the world, even our faith" (I John 5:4).

[7] K. Schilder: *Heaven, What Is It?*, pp. 77-79. Translated and condensed by Marian M. Schoolland. Grand Rapids, Michigan: Eerdmans, 1950.

III

THE DIMENSION OF TIME

A Yale University poet once wrote,

> Because I feel a haughty discontent
> For my gross blemish of mortality,
> I find no joy in any element
> That cannot wash my flesh away from me.[1]

Like many another poet, Johnson disliked the mutability of time; he was not an ascetic in his view of flesh, but simply a man who rebelled against the mortality of matter, and against the fact that time is not eternity suddenly transfixed forever at the point of our desire. Baudelaire also found time to be a horror, declaring, "One must always be drunk, That says it all, There is no other point. In order not to feel the horrible burden of time that bruises your shoulders and bends you to the ground, you must get drunk incessantly." [2] Cummings bewailed the transitoriness of time, writing:

> Eater of all things lovely—Time!
> upon whose watering lips the world
> poises a moment (futile, proud,
> a costly morsel of sweet tears)
> gesticulates, and disappears—[3]

---

[1] Edward Struble Johnson, Jr., "Boy in the Shower Bath," April, 1929, Alfred R. Bellinger editor: *Anthology of Verse from the Yale Literary Magazine*, 1836-1936, p. 133. New Haven: Yale University Press, 1936.

[2] Charles Baudelaire, *The Essence of Laughter*, New York: Meridian Books, 1956, p. 149, cited in William F. Lynch, S.J.: *Christ and Apollo*, p. 49. New York: Mentor-Omega, 1963 (1960).

[3] E. E. Cummings: *Puella Mea*, p. 20. The Golden Eagle Press, 1923.

Cummings' dismay is occasioned by his love of the flesh and his unhappiness at its decay. He wrote:

> if naked flesh she appear to me
> my flesh is an enchanted tree;
> with her lips' most frail parting
> my body hears the cry of Spring,
> and with their frailest syllable
> its leaves go crisp with miracle.[4]

It is "life's very fragile hour" that distressed Cummings.[5] This dismay with time, and the attack upon it, is a result of an over-evaluation of time. When time becomes the primary and determinative order of reality, then time becomes a disappointment. Demands are placed upon time which can only be met by eternity. There is then a hungry demand that time be transfixed and eternalized, and the politics of time-priority works to create a final order, the perfect, unchanging state in order to abolish one aspect of mutability.

The question is therefore one of the relationship of time and eternity. Which is the determinative order? And what is the relationship of eternity to time and to history? Who controls time and history, man or God?

According to the Scripture, God not only created all things, but, before their creation, foreknew because He predestined all things. Not only Romans 8-11, but all of Scripture declares this fact. As the Council of Jerusalem affirmed, "Known unto God are all his works from the beginning of the world" (Acts 15:18). According to Paul, God "worketh all things after the counsel of His will" (Eph. 1:11). The divine decree is universal and all-comprehensive.

The decree includes whatsoever comes to pass in the world, whether it be in the physical or in the moral realm,

[4] *Ibid.*, p. 17.
[5] *Ibid.*, p. 20.

whether it be good or evil, Eph. 1:11. It includes: (a) the good actions of man, Eph. 2:10; (b) their wicked acts, Prov. 16:4; Acts 2:23; 4:27, 28; (c) contingent events, Gen. 45:8; 50:20; Prov. 16:33; (d) the means as well as the end, Ps. 119:89-91; II Thess. 2: 13; Eph. 1:4; (e) the duration of man's life, Job 14:5; Ps. 39:4, and the place of his habitation, Acts 17:26.[6]

Because creation is the work of God, it is determined by God. If the universe is self-generated, if evolution be true, then predestination is impossible, because time is primary and determinative, and eternity is at best a product of time and determined by time. Then man saves himself and man determines his eternal condition by his temporal choice. Creationism and predestination are logical corollaries of each other and cannot logically be separated. Any weakening of creationism is a weakening of predestination and leads to the determination of eternity by time. Arminianism is deeply infected with Hellenic humanism and gives priority, implicity or explicitly, to time over eternity. But if God created man and the universe, then man and the universe are products of God and are determined by Him. The doctrine of evolution, by denying God's creative act, denies also his determination of creation, His predestination of all things. Evolution is scientific Arminianism and asserts the determination of all things by time, a universal self-generation and a possible self-regeneration.

Another consequence haunts every philosophy which abandons creationism and predestination, *magic*. Haroutunian, whose position is hostile to orthodoxy, has noted,

> The crown of Protestant piety is the doctrine of "double election." The notion that God elects some for salvation and others for damnation, which even a theologian like Emil Brunner dismisses as a product of logic rather than piety, is the penultimate produce of the Protestant spirit.

[6] Louis Berkof: *Systematic Theology*, p. 105. Grand Rapids: Eerdmans, 1946.

30

However easily misunderstood (and it has been universally misunderstood!), it represents the virtual liberation of the religion from the anthropocentric perspective, and the delusion, magic, and idolatry it generates. It is the last assertion of God's ultimate freedom as He creates the world, a last terrible tribute to the facts of reprobation as known in this world, a last recognition that one's eternal destiny and one's present status before God are secrets known only to God. It is man's last avowal that the "communication *ad extra*" of God's eternal glory, the "manifestation of his infinite perfections," whether in the good or the evil which life brings to man, even in the sin and death of man, is the "last end for which God created the world." The doctrine of double election, with the implied "willingness to be damned to the glory of God," are essental to Protestant piety. They are iron badges of the Protestant's wisdom, reverence for fact, disinterested love of truth, triumph over self-love in the disinterested love of God.[7]

Neo-orthodox theologians like Haroutunian and Barth use the language of predestination to cover their disbelief in it because they fear the consequences of its abandonment, i.e., sentimental humanism and magic. Their sentimentalism and magic are thus clothed in the language of election, but election and grace reduced to a mythological terminology.

Why the fear of magic, and what is magic? *Magic is the attempt to control and govern the supernatural by means of the natural.* It is thus a belief in the determination of eternity by time. *Arminianism is thus a form of magical theology and belief: it holds that the individual's decision governs eternity.* Man is saved because man chooses Christ. But Jesus declared, "Ye have not chosen me, but I have chosen you" (John 15:16). The primary and determinative choice belongs to the eternal order and the eternal decree.

[7] Joseph Haroutunian: *Wisdom and Folly in Religion*, p. 109f. New York: Charles Scribner's Sons, 1940.

To affirm a belief in the eternal order as prior without at the same time affirming the Biblical doctrine of predestination by the triune God is to destroy the meaning of time without gaining eternity. Platonism and neoplatonism, for example, saw the world of time as a world of shadows, as a world which the wise either rose above or escaped from. But the eternal order, the world of ideas, was not the determinative order, so that, whereas true being belonged to the eternal ideas, true determination belonged to the world of atoms. The result was a schizophrenic and dialectical tension. Increasingly, for many, matter was the horrible, sick and unreal but governing world which a man sought to escape from.

In Christian monasticism, deeply infected by such thinking, the contempt of time and of the world was the prerequisite to holiness and wisdom. Because God was seen as the great Idea, the essence of God's role was not action but to be passively contemplated and adored. Accordingly, "the vision of God" became the goal of time and of history; in other words, the purpose of man in time was to renounce time for vision, which was held to be man's highest good.[8] The triumph of the secular clergy led in part to a rejection of the contempt of time, but the social goal remained the same, the vision of God, and a social order dedicated to it.

The Reformation, by its rejection of Scholasticism and Hellenic thought in favor of Biblical faith, restored the validity of time as God's creation. The offense of the gospel and the sovereignty of God were restored to the faith. The first great intellectual enemy of Christianity, Celsus, had singled out the belief in election as a central offense of Christianity. As Origen reported,

In the next place, ridiculing after his usual style the race

[8] See Kenneth E. Kirk: *The Vision of God, The Christian Doctrine of the Summum Bonum.* London: Longmans, Green, 1931, 1941, second edition.

of Jews and Christians, he compares them all "to a flight
of bats or to a swarm of ants issuing out of their nest, or
to frogs holding council in a marsh, or to worms crawling
together in the corner of a dunghill, and quarrelling with
one another as to which of them were the greater sinners,
and asserting that God shows and announces to us all
things beforehand; and that, abandoning the whole
world, and the regions of heaven, and this great earth,
he becomes a citizen among us alone, and to us alone
makes his intimations, and does not cease sending and
inquiring, in what way we may be associated with him for
ever." And in his fictitious representation, he compares
us to "worms which assert that there is a God, and that
immediately after him, we who are made by him are alto-
gether like unto God, and that all things have been made
subject unto us,—earth, and water, and air, and stars,—
and that all things exist for our sake, and are ordained
to be subject to us." And, according to his representation,
the worms—that is, we ourselves— say that "now, since
certain amongst us commit sin, God will come or will
send his Son to consume the wicked with fire, that the
rest of us may have eternal life with him." [9]

Several very important points appear in Celsus' comment:

1) The early church taught and maintained the doctrine
   of election.

2) God's revelation in Scripture contains predictive
   prophecy by the Lord of history.

3) The persecuted church looked confidently to a victory
   in time and to the subjection of all things, including
   their enemies, to the saints.

4) At the end of time and history, Christ shall come again
   to judge the reprobate and to give eternal life to His
   saints.

The note of victory in time and the importance of time
clearly appear as central to the faith of the early church.

[9] Origen: *Against Celsus*, IV, 23, Ante-Nicene Christian Library,
vol. XXIII, p. 183. Edinburgh: T. & T. Clark, 1872.

A Biblical doctrine of creation under-girded a victorious sense of time in the face of savage persecution.

In Martin Luther's debate with Erasmus, and John Calvin's debate with Pighius, this Biblical note was again introduced into the church.[10] The Biblical declaration of victory is decisive; it rests on the sovereign and creative power of God, and it is openly set forth in the death and resurrection. As Cullmann noted, in the Biblical doctrine of time and history, *"that event on the cross, together with the resurrection which followed, was the already concluded decisive battle."* [11]

The vigor and activism of Protestantism came from this Biblical faith in creation and time. The Kingdom of God became central, not the vision of God. Man enters this Kingdom by grace and then works to further its dominion on earth in the confidence of predestined victory. Because of this responsibility to conquer in the confidence of victory, time is all important and irreplaceable. It is the arena of history and domain of meaning: this is "where the action is." The high compliment Charles Chauncy paid to Cotton Mather was, "He was the greatest redeemer of time I ever knew." [12] This theocentric perspective on time was basic to the colonial and early American eras of American history.[13] Expressive of the activist Protestant attitude towards time is the hymn, "Work, for the night is coming." The time before the end is limited and important: work to

[10] J. J. Packer and O. R. Johnston, translators of Martin Luther: *The Bondage of the Will*, Westwood, New Jersey: Fleming H. Revell, 1957. Henry Cole, translator of John Calvin: *Calvin's Calvinism*, Grand Rapids: Eerdmans, 1950.

[11] Oscar Cullmann: *Christ and Time, The Primitive Christian Conception of Time and History*, p. 84. Philadelphia: Westminster Press, 1950.

[12] Cyclone Covey: The American Pilgrimage, *The Roots of American History, Religion and Culture*, p. 70. New York: Collier, 1961.

[13] H. Richard Niebuhr: *The Kingdom of God in America*. Chicago: Willett, Clark, 1937.

fulfil your destiny; work, saving time. In America especially, this sense of the importance of time has led to a sense of drive and of haste: time cannot be wasted. From the beginning, American inventive genius worked to produce machines in terms of this urgency. The machine had a purpose in terms of time. "Here the machine was not to save labor; it was to save time." [14] Its purpose was thus to increase labor productivity.

This different sense of time made for conflict when Protestant Americans encountered a Roman Catholic culture. In New Orleans, this fact was basic to the triumph of the Know-Nothing Party, which was anti-foreign and anti-Catholic. The Creole (French-Spanish) element in New Orleans had an old-world Catholic orientation, and as a result it despised and regarded with contempt the bustling Americans with their fervor for time-saving, strict schedules, methodical and driving work habits, and their rush to "get ahead" of time. The Americans, similarly, regarded the Creole ways either with horror or with contempt.[15]

The roots of American thrift and practicality are in the American Protestant view of time. Benjamin Franklin simply reflected a secularized version of Cotton Mather's theology; [16] he was a "philosopher" who respected time. Jonathan Edwards and Franklin were both practical men. The American thinkers to 1850 and even later were politicians, churchmen, and men of the world, not academicians. The idea of the university as abstract thought enthroned developed very late in the United States. With Protestantism, everywhere theology moved extensively from the school to the pulpit, although in origin Protestantism was a scholarly

[14] Garet Garrett: *The American Story*, p. 44. Chicago: Regnery, 1955.

[15] See Leon Cyprian Soule: *The Know Nothing Party in New Orleans: A Reappraisal*, p. 7. Published for the Louisiana Historical Association, by Thomas J. Moran's Sons, Baton Rouge, 1961.

[16] Covey, *op. cit.*, p. 80.

cause and crusade. In politics (Milton, James I, etc.), science (Newton), and other areas, the theological mind wrestled with reality rather than abstracting itself from the world.

Thomas Jefferson planned a university in the French (and Catholic) tradition, as a place for abstract thought, but the University of Virginia failed to become that until much later. Jefferson himself was a practical man, although behind many other Americans in this respect.

The Biblical emphasis of Puritanism led to the destruction of the medieval contempt of time which the early Puritans had inherited. In this respect Franklin was closer to the Puritan tradition than Edwards.[17] The monastic, neoplatonistic concept of time infiltrated America in the 18th century through Pietism. As a result, Protestant groups actually established "retreats" from the world of time, cloisters and monastic groups, stressing medieval crafts and adopting monastic garb and celibacy. Ephrata Colony, established by Conrad Beissel, is an example of such movements.

Puritanism held to a this-worldly supernaturalism. The English divine, Richard Baxter, in the Christian Directory (1678), said, "It is action that God is most served and honored by." [18] In America, action and work were highly honored. Rich Americans who wanted to be idle went to Europe, "among whom idleness is still held in honour." As Tocqueville noted, "In the United States, professions are more or less laborious, more or less profitable; but they are never either high or low: every honest calling is honourable."[19]

[17] *Ibid.*, p. 103.
[18] Cited in A. S. P. Woodhouse: *Puritanism and Liberty*, p. (44). London: Dent, 1938.
[19] Alexis De Tocqueville: *Democracy in America*, vol. II, p. 163. New York: Langley, 1841.

This sense of time as the realm of action with victory, in varying degrees characterized Western civilization. The Western powers developed a technological superiority because their faith was one calling for a conquest of history. Their's was a sense of destiny. Imperial armies faced overwhelming forces in the assurance of victory. Time and history were in their favor. In India, the Indian army mutiny of 1857 manifested the conflict of two faiths, one a world and life rejecting view, the other a world and life affirming faith, the one despising time, the other prizing it.

The British won out because, in the long view, they held all the cards in their hands. In a military sense, they had only to hold out until adequate reinforcements became available. After much initial ineptitude, they enjoyed distinguished and resolute leadership from men like the Lawrences and Governor General Canning. Beyond this, the moral factors were on their side. They believed in their right and mission to rule; the tide of Western self-confidence was still flowing strongly. National pride was at its height; death in battle meant a hero's crown; they were the martyrs of the secular religion of the age. But the rebels had no confidence in themselves or their cause. They feared losing something intangible but had no ideas of creating anything new.

Their only positive aims were the restoration of vanished regimes, which would have clashed if they had been revived. In fear and confusion they rose and fought and died. But their deaths were not all in vain, for their failure convinced the quite formless but very real public opinion of India that the way of the old *rajs* could not longer be trodden and that in the future terms must be made with the new forces from the West. Neither Mughal, Maratha, or the Company were the real victor of the struggle. It was the pervasive spirit of the West.[20]

The secularization of the Christian sense of time and

[20] Percival Spear: *India, A Modern History*, p. 272. Ann Arbor: University of Michigan Press, 1961.

destiny led to political and scientific messianism. Salvation and victory were offered through the offices of state and social planners, to whom the power of redeeming the time was ascribed. These secular saviors of time and history have seen themselves as supermen faced with the task of bringing the stupid masses into line. Thus, one scientist remarked, "The supermen built the aeroplane, but the apeman got hold of it." [21]

But without the Christian foundation, even this sense of destiny begins to wane, and the rise of existentialism has steadily eroded the meaning of time and history. As a result, instead of men of time and destiny governing history, history is progressively being dominated by political thugs and vultures who feed on the carcass of civilization. The feast of the vultures will continue until again the mainspring of history is faith in the triune God, until the marriage supper of the Lamb replaces the feast of vultures as the motive force of time. Even as Christ's resurrection set forth His victory over the world of time and matter, so it sets forth His triumph in history, at the center of history and continuously to the end, when there shall be time no longer (Rev. 10:6), and the victories of time culminate in the glory of eternity. Time is not set aside: it is fulfilled and realized. Eternity is the determination and perfection of time; God created time and destines that it culminate in the eternal Kingdom of God. "His servants shall serve him" for the eternal Kingdom is not the perfection of contemplation and vision but of faith and work, and it is expressed in perfect work, free and uncursed (Rev. 22:3).

The Yale poet could find "no joy in any element that cannot wash my flesh away from me" because of its "gross blemish of mortality." The prophet Isaiah was faced with the despairing cry, "All flesh is grass, and all the goodliness

---

[21] John Baillie: *The Belief in Progress*, p. 177. New York: Charles Scribner's Sons, 1951.

thereof is as the flower of the field." His prompt answer was, "The grass withereth, the flower fadeth: but the word of our God shall stand for ever" (Isa. 40:6-8). That word of God gives meaning to every bird, and every blade of grass, so that their appearance in time is purposive and predestined (Matt. 6:26-30). In a universe in which "the very hairs of your head are all numbered" (Matt. 10:30), time has total meaning and total victory, because it is totally determined by the sovereign and triune God.

Note: The foregoing chapters were first delivered at St. Thomas' School, Houston, and first issued as part of the conference papers.

IV

REGENERATION AND HISTORY

Some years ago Westcott observed, "The great mystery of religion is not the punishment, but the forgiveness, of sin: not the natural permanence of Character, but spiritual regeneration." [1] The problem of social and personal regeneration has been a major concern of both religion and philosophy, and the basic conclusions have been clearly pessimistic.

In Oriental and Asiatic thought, especially as it culminates in Indian philosophies, the burden of *Karma* overwhelms history. *Karma* is the effect of any act; every act is a cause creating effects, and man, being a sinner, creates continually a vast burden of effects which reduce history to punishment and life to negation. A pessimistic world and life view thus characterizes such thought. The way of escape is the oblivion of death, *Nirvana*, but even this release is only possible after long ages of reincarnations, during which the burdened soul works out the effects of his *Karma* and is finally released from life. History is thus not only without victory, it is also without meaning, except as a kind of hell or purgatory through which the soul must go in order to escape from this world as well as from life.

The view of reality which such a faith requires is that reality, being, is simply blind, impersonal, unrelenting causality. A cause unleashed can never be cancelled or wiped out: it must simply work itself out through countless ages until

[1] B. B. Westcott: *The Gospel According to St. John*, p. 49, commentary on John 3:5. Grand Rapids: Eerdmans (1881), 1954.

it is totally exhausted. Life consists therefore in exhausting the consequences of *Karma* and avoiding further effects. Asceticism, the forsaking of this blind world of causality and its appetites, is a way of escape. Instead of an affirmation of history, such philosophies are negative towards history, which is the painful world of *Karma*.

Western non-Christian thought has sought to avoid this pessimism by means of dialecticism, but its dialectical philosophies have, regularly since the Greek era, broken down into the same despair of history. The goal of the man who seeks to escape *Karma* is to end history by escape into *Nirvana* or into *Brahma*, to be absorbed into ultimate being and released from time and history. In Western thought, the goal is similarly the end of history, but it is sought differently, the means being *revolution*.

This end-of-history order sought by revolution is a utopian order. It is a world in which the effects of sin and the fall are negated and by-passed. Utopian thinking began as Christianity was by-passed.[2] The Utopia is an end-of-history final order, unchanging and totally controlled. It is still in the world of time, but it negates time by having a final and unchanging order. Modern utopianism dreams also of negating time by overcoming death itself through science.[3] The purpose of revolution is, negatively, the overcoming of causalty and sin in history, the death of history, and, positively, the creation of paradise, the true or Great Community, to use John Dewey's term. Short of revolution, Western non-Christian thought has seen history as cyclical, an endless return of the same frustration by virtue of the same causality. History is like a treadmill: it goes nowhere

[2] See H. Van Riessen: *The Society of the Future*, pp. 38-67, ch. 2, "Utopias." David Hugh Freeman, translator. Philadelphia: Presbyterian and Reformed Publishing Company, 1952.

[3] Robert C. W. Ettinger: *The Prospect of Immortality*. Garden City, New York: Doubleday, 1964.

fast. The answer is seen as the destruction of history by revolution.

It was such problems as these that Nicodemus raised with Jesus: what hope was there for man in history? The answer of Jesus was direct: "Verily, verily, I say unto thee, Except a man be born again, he cannot see the Kingdom of God" (John 3:3). To Nicodemus this seemed incredible: "How can a man be born when he is old? Can he enter the second time into his mother's womb, and be born?" (John 3:4). The point raised by Nicodemus was a penetrating one: how can a man, whose personality is so deeply his history, cancel that history? Short of returning to his mother's womb, i.e., undoing and negating his whole history, dropping it miraculously into non-existence, how can man be regenerated? Bishop Wescott ably summarized Nicodemus' implicit thesis:

> How is it possible for a man whose whole nature at any moment is the sum of all the past, to start afresh? How can he undo, or do away with, the result which years have brought and which goes to form himself? His "I" includes the whole development through which he has passed; and how then can it survive a new birth? Can the accumulation of long ages be removed and the true "self" remain? [4]

Implicit in this perspective is the belief that a man is his history, the sum total of his past, and that the causality of history is from within history. This is environmentalism, a belief that the individual, the race, and history are products of their environment, are effects rather than causes, causality belonging to the environment rather than man. Man becomes an effect, a product, and causality is primarily ascribed to the environment rather than to God, for Christian faith ascribes it to God, and then to man under God.

"Jesus answered, Verily, verily, I say unto thee, Except a

[4] Wescott: *Comm. on St. John*, p. 49, comm. *ad. loc.*

42

man be born of water and of the Spirit, he cannot enter into the Kingdom of God" (John 3:5). The *water* signifies forgiveness of sins, purification, as set forth in baptism. The past is not destroyed; forgiveness covers it, and the totality of the past is now put to good, our good and God's glory (Rom. 8:28). The *Spirit* means that man's regeneration is the act of God the Holy Spirit, Who regenerates man into the perfect humanity of Jesus Christ. The work of regeneration is not destructive but regenerative. God so loved the world, His creation (John 3:16), that He is re-creating it by saving men, a first step towards "the times of restitution of all things" (Acts 3:21).

Non-Christian philosophies must work to destroy history, to end history or to escape it. They make time primary but they cannot honor it. They make history more basic than eternity and then seek to escape the hell their history has become.

The doctrine of the forgiveness of sins destroys the necessity for subservience to *Karma*, the cyclical view of history, and the pessimism of all non-Christian philosophies. Regeneration means the introduction of a new creation into history. It means that Christ, the new man and last Adam, the fountain-head of the new humanity, is the source of the new society. Society cannot be saved by environmentalism, by the futile manipulation of externals as the means of salvation. Such a perspective involves a radical pessimism concerning man and history. The doctrine of regeneration declares God's respect for His creation. The destiny of creation is regeneration and fulfilment in terms of God's creative purpose and eternal decree. History is not destroyed nor time despised but rather redeemed. Torrance has summarized the victorious spontaneity of the New Testament believer:

There is no anxious concern about the past. It is Christ

43

that died! There is no anxious striving toward an ideal. It is Christ that rose again! In Him all the Christian's hopes are centred. His life is hid with Christ in God. In Him a new order of things has come into being, by which the old is not set aside.[5]

Without regeneration, history is inescapably caught in the tension of hopeless despair and the impossibility of flight.

[5] Thomas F. Torrance: *The Doctrine of Grace in the Apostolic Fathers*, p. 34f. Grand Rapids: Eerdmans, 1949.

V

THE CONCEPT OF AN ULTIMATE DECREE

If tomorrow the word and idea of "life" were abolished from all languages, and men forbidden to allude to "life," it might have an effect on speech, but it would not alter life and reality in the slightest. Men would, by other terms, continue to speak of "life" and to live it. Similarly, the general distaste for the word and idea of "predestination" no more affects reality than the abolition of "life." The idea of predestination is an inescapable concept. It is a premise of all human thinking, a logical concomitant to thinking. The universe moves in terms of God's eternal decree, and man, created in God's image, thinks inevitably in terms of the purpose, pattern, and decree which predestination gives to all creation and to the functions of human thought.

When man therefore denies the divine predestination, he denies God's eternal decree only to replace it with another decree. With the Enlightenment, men rebelled against the sovereign and triune God, and, while retaining Him formally as Creator or First Cause, replaced Him in essence with the concept of Nature. Nature became the source of law, and natural law replaced revelation as the norm for religion and society. An eternal decree was ascribed to Nature, whereby all things had a totality of meaning which made this the best of all possible worlds. Pope gave poetical expression to this faith:

All Nature is but art, unknown to thee;

45

All chance, direction, which thou canst not see;
All discord, harmony not understood;
A partial evil, universal good:
And, spite of pride, in erring reason's spite,
One truth is clear, WHATEVER IS, IS RIGHT.[1]

To make Nature the source of a valid eternal decree, it was necessary to abolish the Fall from Nature. After all, how could Nature be the source of ultimate truth and final law if Nature represented only a fallen and sin-ridden order? Thus, a second aspect of the decree appears: *first*, the concept of predestination is a basic aspect of whatever is ultimate in any system, and, *second*, inerrancy is a logical concomitant of ultimacy. What is ultimate is simply ultimate: there is no other truth, like it or not, and, in terms of itself, since the ultimate can only and always be true to itself, it is inerrant and infallible. Whatever becomes ultimate in any system becomes inevitably inerrant and infallible, even though men prefer to avoid those terms because of their Christian connotations.

When, however, Nature was subjected to evolutionary theory, the concept of an infallible Nature, natural law, and a divine decree within Nature, was shattered. Nature represented simply, in Darwinism, chance and natural selection. Darwin tried to read a decree into this operation, but the damage was done. Another locale for the divine decree was necessary: Nature was another dead god gone down the drain.

In terms of the new perspective of evolution, truth and meaning do not exist in the universe. In other words, there is no decree inherent in the universe or behind the universe. Man is alone, an accident of being, in a cold and alien universe which is the product of the fortuitous concourse of atoms. In this situation, man feels that he must do two things to survive. *First*, he must renounce the luxury and

[1] Alexander Pope: *An Essay on Man*, Epistle I, x.

46

insanity of assuming that a god or gods exist. He must face the universe of brute factuality coldly and starkly. *Second,* truth and meaning are purely human categories of thought. They are man's creations and must be imposed on the universe. Man must now control and guide evolution; he must use the universe and master himself as well. A decree is necessary, and it does not exist in or behind the universe: man must therefore promulgate his own divine decree and impose it upon human society and upon all creation. The instruments of man's decree are *science and the state;* brought together, they mean scientific socialism, a society planned by a scientific elite, social engineers or social scientists.

The impact of Darwinism forced this necessity to locate a new source for ultimate law and decree on all facets of Western thought which accepted the theory of evolution. Prior to Darwin, of course, social evolution was already a widely held premise of Western thought, especially among those under the influence of Hegel.

Four approaches to the crisis can be briefly cited. First, the Marxist approach very quickly manifested its contempt of truth and meaning. Marx and Engels noted that Communism was accused of denying "eternal truths, such as Freedom, Justice, etc., that are common to all states of society. . . . Communism abolishes eternal truths, it abolishes all religion, and all morality, instead of constituting them on a new basis; it therefore acts in contradiction to all past historical experience." Marx and Engels, instead of denying this charge, simply declared that all such "truths" were simply reflections of material circumstances, i.e., economically conditioned.

> The charges against communism made from a religious, a philosophical, and, generally, from an ideological standpoint, are not deserving of serious examination.

Does it require deep intuition to comprehend that man's ideas, views, and conceptions, in one word, man's consciousness, changes with every change in the conditions of his material existence, in his social relations and in his social life?

What else does the history of ideas prove, than that intellectual production changes its character in proportion as material production is changed? The ruling ideas of each age have ever been the ideas of its ruling class.[2]

The one reality is a "process of eternal change," and even man's reason is invalid as it confronts this process. As a prominent Marxist has stated it,

> *Thus dialectics teaches that at each instant in time and in each point in space something is born and evolves, something dissolves and disappears. What appears stable has already begun to die; and from its death life is born. It is an endless process of motion.*

This process of eternal change in things obeys rules which are not those of Aristotle's logic. Since Aristotle, the principle of contradiction has dominated the reasoning of philosophers: "A thing," they said, "cannot at the same time be and not be." But it can! Being contains its opposite within itself. It is itself transformed. That which appears unstable is destined to die under the influence of contrary forces. The present is explained by the past, in which it was already contained. One cannot understand it unless one knows whence it comes.[3]

Since truth is non-existent, the purpose of philosophy must not be *meaning* but *control*. As Marx wrote,

> X. The standpoint of the old materialism is "civil" society; the standpoint of the new is *human* society, or socialized humanity.

[2] Karl Marx and Frederick Engels, "Manifesto of the Communist Party" in *On Religion*, p. 88f. Moscow: Foreign Languages Publishing House, 1955.

[3] Marcel Cachin: *Science and Religion*, p. 19f. New York: International Publishers, 1946.

XI. The philosophers have only *interpreted* the world, in various ways; the point, however is to *change* it.[4]

This scientific socialism is man's decree of predestination applied to history, to man and society, in order to give a "human" meaning to society. Man is thus sacrificed to the totalitarian state, to the scientific planners, as the only means of securing a decree and meaning in history.

A second approach to the crisis has been that of American pragmatism, whose notable figures have been C. S. Peirce, William James, and John Dewey. C. S. Peirce defined pragmatism to say in effect that the meaning of any proposition is its logical or physical consequence. "In order to ascertain the meaning of an intellectual conception one should consider what practical consequences might conceivably result by necessity from the truth of that conception; and the sum of these consequences will constitute the entire meaning of the conception." Again, Peirce stated, "Pragmatism is the principle that every theoretical judgment expressible in a sentence in the indicative mood is a confessed form of thought whose only meaning, if it has any, lies in its tendency to enforce a corresponding practical maxim expressible as a conditional sentence having its apodosis in the imperative mood."[5] "Truth," we might say, is thus whatever works, and William James, in *Pragmatism,* in essence so defined it. Truth is thus functional or instrumental, not metaphysical. Metaphysics and religion, after Comte, belong to an earlier and more primitive phase of man's history. The concern of science is *not with truth but method,* and hence methodology is a major concern. The problem of science is thus the best method of attaining that social order in which scientific planning, prediction and

[4] Karl Marx, "Theses on Feuerbach," in *On Religion*, p. 72.
[5] Vernon J. McGill, "Pragmatism," in Dagobert D. Runes: *Dictionary of Philosophy*, p. 245. New York: Philosophical Library, 1960.

control, can be best used to organize man into a state most conducive to his welfare as it is scientifically determined. The new decree is thus a product of the scientific control of human society by means of science in the Great Society, in order to produce the Great Community.

Fabian Socialism gives us a third approach to the crisis. Like the other strands in modern thought, it substitutes predestination by the sovereign socialist state for predestination by the sovereign and triune God. Fabianism retained in part the old liberal illusion that there could be a union of "the greatest individual liberty" with "common ownership" or socialism.[6] Whereas Marxism broke with the ostensibly bourgeois concept of liberty, Fabianism, while equally socialistic, maintained that the old liberty would find its fulfilment in the new socialism, although this hope has come progressively to be more and more a cynical facade. Moreover, Fabianism, because of its radical relativism, felt it unnecessary to maintain the theoretical apparatus of Marxism. It therefore by-passed three basic ideas of Marxism. First, it dropped the materialistic or economic interpretation of history. No other concept was substituted, because no theoretical framework was desired: the emphasis is on present planning and control. Second, the concept of the class struggle was dropped, and, third, the surplus value theory was discarded. To be a Marxist requires some intensive study of Marx and Engels. To be a Fabian requires nothing more than a belief in scientific socialism. There is no body of thought to which one must subscribe. The Fabian position is an intellectual posture of cynicism for all modes of thinking save those which reach Fabian conclusions, which approve, in brief, Fabian policies. As a result, Fabian Socialism has had a great appeal for many people, including clergymen. It involves no intelligence,

[6] *Autobiography of John Stuart Mill*, p. 168. Foreword by Asa Briggs. New York: New American Library, 1964.

50

no identifying party membership, and no real responsibility for anything save a subscription to socialism. As a logically relativistic philosophy, it is in essence anti-intellectual and basically congenial to irrationalism in the name of science. A fourth approach to the crisis is neo-orthodoxy. Neo-orthodoxy is that form of existentialist philosophy which uses the concepts of orthodox Christianity and of theology as the tools of an alien system, existentialism. Van Til has called attention to this aspect of Karl Barth's thinking:

> In all this opposition to the idea of revelation as directly identical with history, Barth is doing, in effect, what Kierkegaard did when he argued that truth is in the Subject.
>
> Barth tells us that a true approach to theology must be existential. But a true existential approach is not possible on the basis of the idea of direct revelation. On the basis of objective or direct revelation, man is not really involved in the question of his relation to God. "Where the question is really that pertaining to man, there the subjective is the objective." [7]

Neo-orthodoxy, like Marxism, pragmatism, Fabianism, and existentialism, is a product of Kantianism, and for Kant man is the ultimate source of all law and hence of the only decree and determination possible in history. All these, and other modern systems, are developments of Kantianism, and they agree, first, in denying God's revelation and His eternal decree. Second, they reject the 18th century concept of a decree within Nature. Third, they agree in insisting on man's decree as the necessary decree in order to establish meaning in history. Fourth, they are thus all totalitarian and socialistic, closer to one another than to Christianty, against which they are uniformly hostile. Fifth, political liberalism logically involves and presupposes re-

[7] Cornelius Van Til: *Christianity and Barthianism*, p. 309. Philadelphia: Presbyterian & Reformed Publishing Company, 1962.

ligious liberalism. The premise of both is the substitution of the sovereignty of man in the person of the state for the sovereignty of God. Political and religious liberalism both deny God's decree to establish man's decree via the state. Marxism to a degree, and especially pragmatism, Fabianism, and neo-orthodoxy are forms of existentialism. Van Til has called attention, in his analysis of James Daane's thinking, to the difference between Biblical thinking and existentialism:

Reformed theology thinks of Scripture as a directly discernible expression of the will of God for man. Modern existentialism, on the other hand, is based on the idea that human experience makes its norms and ideas as it moves. For it "to exist" involves knowing nothing in the way of absolute truth.[8]

James Daane, in attacking Van Til in *A Theology of Grace*, specifically attacked him for "making God's eternal decrees his point of departure."[9] Daane continues then to establish an existential foundation for his theology. In Van Til's summary, "Daane assumes, with Kierkegaard, that finite existence is a concept that must be defined independently of God. It cannot be defined in terms of the plan of God."[10]

It is not surprising, in view of Daane's position, that *The Reformed Journal*, and the movement both Daane and the *Journal* represent, should be hostile to constitutional conservatism and very congenial to the Fabian establishment in Washington, D. C. Politically and theologically, it represents a transition from faith in God's eternal decree to the decree of the scientific planners.

Existentialism, however, does not stand still; like pregnancy, it moves ahead towards its logical conclusion. Van

[8] Cornelius Van Til: *The Defense of the Faith*, p. 214. Philadelphia: Presbyterian and Reformed Publishing Company, 1955.
[9] James Daane: *A Theology of Grace*, p. 24. Grand Rapids: Eerdmans, 1954.
[10] Van Til, *op. cit.*, p. 417.

Til has pointed out that human experience is normative for existentialism. Von Fersen has said of existential philosophy that it

Determines the worth of knowledge not in relation to truth but according to its biological value contained in the pure data of consciousness when unaffected by emotions, volitions, and social prejudice. Both the source and the elements of knowledge are sensations as they "exist" in our consciousness. There is no difference between the external and internal world, as there is no natural phenomenon which could not be examined psychologically; it all has its "existence" in states of the mind. . . .

It is strictly non-metaphysical, anti-hypothetical, and contends to give only a simple description of existent psychological realities.[11]

Existentialism is thus a philosophy which denies any idea of ultimate truth when it is consistently held. For existentialism, knowledge has no relationship to truth; an idea is knowledge, not because it is true but if it is useful in terms of our biological demands, or, to use Von Fersen's phrase, it is valid knowledge "according to its biological value contained in the pure data of consciousness when unaffected by emotions, volitions, and social prejudices."

In other words, the only criterion of any idea or knowledge is how it affects us when we think purely as animals, without any religious, moral, or social prejudices. Nihilists and beatniks are thus consistent existentialists.

Fabianism, like pragmatism and Marxism, thus approaches society with this framework of reference. Accordingly, a first premise of Fabian, pragmatist, and Marxist politics is that there is no truth, only expediency. There is no evil involved in a political program: only success or

[11] Sigmar Von Fersen, "Existential Philosophy," in D. D. Runes: *Dictionary of Philosophy*, p. 102f.

failure in terms of the socialist purpose, man's control of man and the universe, man's own decree as ultimate law. Truth therefore is what works, and a lie may be the best truth in operation. Second, there is no law beyond the state, no ultimate truth in the universe. The state therefore cannot err, because there is no law in terms of which the state can be judged except itself. The state is thus in error only when it deems it: Stalin erred only when Khrushchev said he did; similarly, Khrushchev erred only when his successors said that he did. There is no appeal against the existential moment. Every social order that becomes existentialist thereby progressively denies and ultimately destroys all possibility of appeal against the moment, because the uninvolved biology of the moment is its own truth.

Neo-orthodoxy operates with a similar framework of reference. First, it has, implicitly or explicitly, no truth, no word, outside of man. Neo-orthodoxy uses the Biblical word as the symbol or sign for the totally human word. It negates the historicity of the Bible by insisting that the Bible is a dialectical rather than a theistic book. Thus, Niebuhr holds:

> In reinterpreting the New Testament idea of the *parousia* (and, as we shall see later, all other ideas dealing with the relation of history and super-history, such as resurrection and judgment) it is important to take Biblical symbols seriously but not literally. If they are taken literally the Biblical conception of a dialectical relation between history and super-history is imperiled; for in that case the fulfillment of history becomes merely another kind of time-history. If the symbols are not taken seriously the Biblical dialectic is destroyed, because in that case concepts of an eternity are connoted in which history is destroyed and not fulfilled.[12]

[12] Reinhold Niebuhr: *The Nature and Destiny of Man, A Christian Interpretation*, vol. II, p. 50. New York: Charles Scribner's Sons, 1943.

Thus, for Niebuhr there is no infallible word nor any possibility of it, because there is no sovereign and triune God Whose infallible and eternal decree governs all creation and Who therefore can speak authoritatively and finally on all subjects. An infallible Scripture requires and presupposes an eternal decree, because only a God Who totally governs all history can speak without error concerning it. For Niebuhr there is thus no authoritative word, no real truth about history. Hence Niebuhr is a strong advocate of a tolerance of all kinds of ideas and theologies, because no authoritative word or final truth has been spoken whereby men and ideas can be judged.[13] Thus life is basically meaningless in itself. Niebuhr has tried to avoid the existentialist conclusion that life is an absolute absurdity by stating, "The final truth about life is always an absurdity but it cannot be an absolute absurdity. It is an absurdity insofar as it must transcend the 'system' of meaning which the human mind always prematurely constructs with itself at the centre."[14] Howard has noted of Niebuhr:

Careful scrutiny reveals that Niebuhr's final authority for his theological affirmations is frequently nothing more than the subjective feelings of the believer. Thus, in a much more complex manner than William James, his theology reduces itself to James' pragmatism: if faith makes one feel better, it is true for that person.[15]

Niebuhr's one area of bitter intolerance is for those who hold to the infallible word: this for him is the great sin of pride. Since he admits no infallible word, to hold to one is a profession of pride, not of faith.

Second, for Niebuhr also there is thus no law beyond man in this essentially absurd universe. For him also the state

[13] *Ibid.*, II, pp. 213-243.
[14] *Ibid.*, II, p. 38.
[15] Irving Howard, "Reinhold Niebuhr, Apostle of Power," in *Christian Economics*, vol. VIII, no. 19, October 30, 1956, p. 4.

is the source of law and of the inescapable decree. He is thus, in Howard's phrase, an apostle of power, of statist power. Niebuhr, well aware of the pitfalls of his position, has tried to make his view of political power a cynical one. He has written on *The Illusion of World Government*,[16] but he is still an advocate of the United Nations and of socialism. Short of suicide, he has nowhere else to go. Either man accepts the sovereign God and His eternal decree, or man will establish in history his own sovereign authority and decree. In Niebuhr's system, the state is viewed cynically, but there is no law or appeal beyond the state.

In such perspectives, ultimacy is given to the state, and the only morality for the state is the successful use of power. For individuals, the "new" morality of existentialism and of all modern schools of thought is simply freedom from God's law. Meland's principle is that "Freedom is obedience to self-formulated rules," and he urges us to write our "own ten commandments." [17] In Meland's own formulation of "a modern man's ten commandments," there is no law, only self-fulfilment.[18]

The ostensible morality of this post-Kantian world is "love." There is no moral law in personal matters for this tradition other than love. But "love," in any historic and realistic sense, is a strong devotion and adherence to someone or something, together with a separation in terms of that love, and an aversion of or hatred for its opposite. Love is thus linked with hate. Such love is despised by these post-Kantians. With respect to mother love, Edith de Rham has called it "the love fraud" and advocates the placing of babies in group situations and nurseries after the pattern of Russia, Israel, and Sweden.[19]

[16] Published in 1949 by The Graphics Group, Whitestone, New York.
[17] Bernard Eugene Meland: *Write Your Own Ten Commandments*, Chicago: Willett, Clark, 1938.
[18] *Ibid.*, p. 71f.
[19] Edith de Rham: *The Love Fraud, Why the Structure of the*

"Love" in the "new" morality is simply the total tolerance of all evil. A prominent leader in this school of thought was the humanist, Albert Schweitzer, whose only moral principle was "reverence for life," which meant the total acceptance of all life irrespective of moral and religious principles. Schweitzer thus in effect demanded the toleration of all evil, which means also the total intolerance of all righteousness, because righteousness is intolerant, and it seeks to redeem a fallen world and eradicate the consequences of sin.

This "morality" is the age-old standard of occultism and of various subversive groups. It was the creed of the self-styled "Beast," Aleister Crowley, whose doctrine, by no means original with him, was "Do what thou wilt shall be the whole law. Love is the law." [20]

The conclusion of all these post-Kantian systems is in the exaltation of the state and the supplanting of God's eternal decree with the totalitarian decree of the state. To restore liberty to the world of man and to history it is necessary to restore the doctrine of the eternal decree of the sovereign and triune God. Far from destroying man's liberty, the doctrine of predestination is the only valid foundation for it. In the words of the Westminster Confession of Faith (ch. III, sec. I):

> God from all eternity did by the most wise and holy counsel of his own will, freely and unchangeably ordain whatsoever comes to pass: yet so as thereby neither is God the author of sin, nor is violence offered to the will of the creatures, nor is the liberty or contingency of second causes taken away, but rather established.

Upon this foundation the liberty of Christendom has been established. It cannot exist on any other premise.

American Family Is Changing and What Women Must Do to Make It Work. New York: Clarkson N. Potter, 1965.

[20] *Inquire Within: Trail of the Serpent*, p. 261. London: Boswell, 1936.

VI

ETERNALIZING TIME

Throughout history, men have often been in rebellion against eternity, but they have been no less in rebellion against time. They resent eternity, because it is beyond them, and they resent time, because it is not eternity. Accordingly, men have repeatedly attempted to eternalize time, to arrest history, by creating an unchanging society which is a "final order."

One means by which men have attempted to arrest history has been the family. The classic example of this is Tibetan polyandry. By means of polyandry, the Tibetan society, prior to the Communist conquest, maintained an unchanging social order. The purpose was to retain property intact and society in a stable, continuing, and unchanging order. The eldest son inherited the property in its entirety and the problem of fractional heirship was avoided. The younger sons who did not become lamas had to share in the eldest son's wife and estate to live. Sometimes the brothers took more than one woman as their joint wives, but, irrespective of the number of joint wives and joint husbands, the eldest son inherited all, and the property was handed on intact. This system was by no means productive of peace or harmony. It was definitely conducive to clashes and to unhappiness. Even Justice Douglas, who is prone to see good in all things, observed, "I learned that the polyandry system breeds prostitution." [1]

[1] William Orville Douglas: *Beyond the High Himalayas*, p. 183. Garden City, New York: Doubleday, 1952.

What polyandry in Tibet did produce was a social equilibrium at the cost of peace, character, and progress. An unchanging order was the goal, a society to reflect the quality of eternity. But men die, and, before they die, they grow old, so that men change and cannot therefore reflect this unchanging quality of eternity. Mutability is inescapably a part of man's physical nature. If therefore time and history are to be immobilized, it must be the social order which is immobilized and rendered unchanging, because people will age and perish. As a result, whenever and wherever time is eternalized, man is sacrificed to the social order. The unchanging order must remain, and it must be paramount, and changing man must be sacrificed to it. In Tibetan polyandry, the personal goals of the sons were irrelevant: either they conformed to the land and marriage system or they conformed to the Buddhist monastic system. Similarly, the wishes of the wife had no standing: she was required to be the wife of all the brothers to preserve the unchanging social order and its land system. That many men and women were in friction goes without saying, but that none revolted and altered the system is equally true. The system was eternal, unchanging, and who was changing man to rebel against eternity?

Other family systems in ancient and more recent societies have sought to eternalize time. Ancestor worship linked the supernatural and eternal order to the family. The worship of ancestors had a doubly paralyzing effect on history. *First*, ancestor worship linked a sinful human order to eternity in irrevocable union, so that an area of life which should be *under* the law and judgment of eternity became the incarnation of the eternal order. *Second*, the family still remained in time, in history, and ancestor worship gave the family a deadly historical perspective, the backward look. Instead of progress, retrogression was the law.

The state has had a similar history. Many early forms of the state were believed to be the mystical bond or union of heaven and earth. The ruler or the state represented the presence of the eternal order in time. History was immobilized in terms of this immanent will of the gods, and a backward look prevailed.

With the Renaissance and the Enlightenment, Utopian thought began to posit a future order, an unchanging society and final state for man. In this ideal order, the idea of history will become flesh; the idea will take full form. The dialectic of history, in this philosophy, is a clash between form and matter, nature and freedom, thesis and antithesis, and with the synthesis the realization will come. Accordingly, the goal of history has become the death of history. God and eternity are denied, but time and history are also denied, in that they must be transcended and history must be eternalized.

Utopianism is an aspect of all socialist thinking, Marxist, Fabian and "Christian," and of "welfare economics" as well. The political goal offered to men is a final order, the solution to man's problems. This final order is only delayed by certain "reactionary" elements who either oppose utopianism or have another form of utopianism to offer. Overwhelm and destroy this dissident element, by education or liquidation, and utopia will arrive: such is the thesis, and basic to this faith is a hatred of man and of history, a hatred of time and of eternity.

From the Biblical perspective, time is time: it involves and requires change and decay, progress and problems, movement and counter-movement. Even before the fall, there was a time and history in Eden. Adam and Eve aged markedly more slowly but they were daily a little older. Trees budded, burst forth with blossoms, gave fruit, and then dropped their leaves. Man's mandate was to exercise dominion over the earth (Gen. 1:28), and this was a task requiring time and having an historical prospect.

Marriage, ordained in paradise, had time and history in view. Because history is movement, it entails birth, maturity and death. Each generation fulfills its destiny, and another resumes the pilgrimage of history, which is man's destiny and privilege. When God instituted marriage in Eden, before any parents existed, He ordained, "Therefore shall a man leave his father and his mother, and shall cleave unto his wife: and they shall be one flesh" (Gen. 2:24). The significance of this verse is very great. The past must be honored; honoring parents involves sometimes their support economically, as needed. But a man must *leave* his father and mother and *cleave* unto his wife. He must break with the one institution to create another. The old must be honored, but history must move forward. The old authority is honored at God's very specific commandment (Deut. 5:16), but the honor of the old requires the creation of the new authority. The new husband must establish his own area of dominion in family and calling. The unchanging authority is not of this world: it is the sovereign and triune God and His revealed and infallible word. Man belongs to time and to history, and, as long as he is in time, he must remain in history. It is the perversity of sin which makes men denounce heaven and eternity, and then work to negate time and history by trying to convert it into heaven. The result is hell on earth.

From the Biblical perspective, time is not eternalized: it is redeemed from the fall (Eph. 5:16; Col. 4:5) and made the arena of man's dominion. Instead of being bewailed, time is to be enjoyed under God, for, according to the Catechism, man's chief end is to glorify God and to enjoy Him forever: this is man's role in time and eternity. Even in the midst of tribulation, the note of joy must resound: "Rejoice in the Lord alway: and again I say, Rejoice"

(Phil. 4:4), because time and history witness not only movement and struggle but also the inescapable victory of God's people (I John 5:4).

Attempts of various men, such as Harvey Cox in *The Secular City* (1965), to secularize history go hand in hand with an attempt to incarnate a revolutionary idea in history and thereby arrest history. Cox calls it "The Church's Koinonio Function: Making Visible the City of Man."[2] But the City of Man does not arrest history or realize it: it merely produces the chaos of revolution.

The essence of such positions is the rebellion against the sovereign God and His eternal decree, against the predetermination of history and time by eternity. But, since time and history are themselves the creation of the triune God, every rejection of God involves also a rejection of His creation as well and an attempt to force a new creation on an assumed world of ostensibly brute factuality. The consequence is a rejection of time and history and the mad shambles of the City of Man.

[2] Harvey Cox: *The Secular City*, p. 144. New York: Macmillan, 1965.

VII

TRUTH AND HISTORICAL ACTION

The critical question, "What is truth?," is basic to every culture and civilization. Every civilization rests on an answer, explicit or implicit, to the question of truth, and every culture is a conception of truth externalized. The life of a culture is its "truth," and it prospers or falls in terms of the nature of that faith.

At the end of every age, when the foundations of a civilization are decaying and disappearing, the question of truth ceases to be an academic exercise and becomes a problem for survival. Various ideas of truth compete to command the future. Every idea becomes a live option in the market-place of survival, but not every idea is a promise of survival. In order to understand the conflicting concepts of truth, it is necessary to cite and distinguish the major contenders for man's mind and future.

First, a prominent force in history has been the concept of truth as formulated by *rationalism*, both in the East and in the West. In this perspective, truth is an idea, an ideal, the form or the reality of being. The influence of this concept on Asian history is very great, although it is best known for its Hellenic formulation and subsequent history. Depending upon the particular variation of this rationalism, the result is a down-grading and contempt for a particular segment of reality. In Plato's *Republic*, the "truth" is the idea of the total state and man's unity therein. Individuality or particularity belong to the world of matter and are thus lesser in significance and therefore only "find" themselves as they are subject to the "truth," the totalitarian order of Plato's dream.

On the other hand, when spirit as the truth is pitted against matter, the consequence of this rationalism is mysticism and asceticism. The untrue world of matter or illusion must be transcended for the true world of spirit or form.

In another form, this rationalism sees the truth or form of being as a changing, developing process. Eric Voegelin, in *Order and History* (3 v.), speaks of the periodic "leaps in being." Each "leap in being" is an unfolding of the new and developing, and also changing, course of being. Voegelin's position is thus an ultimate relativism. The next "leap in being" can be a reversal of present-day truth, so that "God" in a sense is present only in the victorious movements of history. That Voegelin has been hailed by some *National Review* writers as a great conservative is an excellent indication of the intellectual bankruptcy of these scholars.

Other variations of rationalism exist. Its influences on the political left and right are many. One notable "conservative" exponent of rationalism of a neo-platonic form was Richard M. Weaver, author of *Ideas Have Consequences*, *The Ethics of Rhetoric*, and *Visions of Order*.

In every form, however, rationalism, because it overtaxes and over-evaluates reason, is destructive of reason. The observation often made by Cornelius Van Til, that rationalism always ends in irrationalism, describes a fact abundantly in evidence in the history of thought.

A *second* approach to truth is that of Edmund Burke's followers. It rests in great measure on a concept which appears in one of Burke's most famous passages:

Society is, indeed, a contract. Subordinate contracts for objects of mere occasional interest may be dissolved at pleasure; but the state ought not to be considered as nothing better than a partnership agreement in a trade of pepper and coffee, calico or tobacco, or some other such low concern, to be taken up for a little temporary interest, and to be dissolved by the fancy of the parties. It is to be looked on with other reverence; because it is not a partnership in things subservient only to the gross animal existence of a temporary and perishable nature. It is a partnership in all science, a partnership in all art, a partnership in every virtue and in all perfection. As the ends of such a partnership cannot be obtained in many generations, it becomes a partnership, not only between those who are living, but between those who are living, those who are dead, and those who are to be born. Each contract of each particular state is but a clause in the great primeval contract of eternal society, linking the lower with the higher natures, connecting the visible and invisible world, according to a fixed compact sanctioned by the inviolable oath which holds all physical and all moral natures each in their appointed place. This law is not subject to the will of those who, by an obligation above them, and infinitely superior, are bound to submit their will to that law. The municipal corporations of that universal kingdom are not morally at liberty, at their pleasure, and on their speculations of a contingent improvement, wholly to separate and tear asunder the bands of their subordinate community, and to dissolve it into an unsocial, uncivil, unconnected chaos of elementary principles. It is the first and supreme necessity only a necessity that is not chosen, but chooses, a necessity paramount to deliberation, that admits no discussion and demands no evidence, which alone can justify a resort to anarchy. This necessity is no exception to the rule; because this necessity itself is a part, too, of that moral and physical disposition of things to which man must be obedient by consent or force: but if that which is only submission to necessity should be made the object of choice, the law is broken, Nature is disobeyed, and the rebellious are outlawed, cast forth, and exiled, from this world of reason, and order, and peace, and virtue, and

65

fruitful penitence, into the antagonistic world of madness, discord, vice, confusion, and unavailing sorrow.[1]

It is important to note, however, that while Burke emphasized the significance of tradition and continuity for political health, he subordinated all things to the authority and truth of God. As he told his electors on November 3, 1774,

> Certainly, Gentlemen, it ought to be the happiness and glory of a representative to live in the strictest union, the closest correspondence, and the most unreserved communication with his constituents. Their wishes ought to have great weight with him; their opinions high respect; their business unremitted attention. It is his duty to sacrifice his repose, his pleasure, his satisfactions, to theirs,—and above all, ever, and in all cases, to prefer their interest to his own.

> But his unbiased opinion, the mature judgment, his enlightened conscience, he ought not to sacrifice to you, to any man, or to any set of men living. These he does not derive from your pleasure,—no, nor from the law and the Constitution. They are a trust from Providence, for the abuse of which he is deeply answerable. Your representative owes you, not his industry only, but his judgment; and he betrays, instead of serving you, if he sacrifices it to your opinion.[2]

Hallowell has well summarized the weaknesses of Burke's position, and with charity:

> Undoubtedly Burke placed greater reliance upon the redemptive power of history as such than history can or does warrant. He conceived of God as a kind of divine immanence working in history for the redemption of mankind but he neglected the conception of God as a

[1] *The Works of the Right Honorable Edmund Burke*, vol. III, p. 359f., "Reflections on the Revolution in France." Sixth Edition. Boston: Little, Brown, 1880.

[2] *Ibid.*, vol. II, p. 95, "Speech to the Electors of Bristol, Nov. 3, 1774."

transcendent Being confronting each one of us here and now. The Church, he conceived more in terms of its utility as a social institution than as a divine institution for the mediation of grace.

It was not Burke's intention, however, to develop either a systematic political philosophy or a theology. His ideas were formulated in response to specific political events, in the heat of battle and in his role as statesman. If he transcended the role of statesman to utter some truths of timeless quality we may be grateful, that, however unsystematic as a thinker, he combined the talents of a politician with the wisdom of a philosopher. And that was as rare a combination in his day as it is in ours.[3]

Burke's perspective was political, not philosophical. His contemporary academic followers too often take the purely political and exalt it into a philosophical premise. In the hands of Kirk, the pragmatic and political necessity and reality of continuity and tradition, and a respect for it, become "the principle of continuity," a basic premise of thought. Kirk writes:

Burke, then, spoke with the authority of a profound and practical intellect, not merely with the enthusiasm of an accomplished rhetorician, when he described the great primaeval contract of eternal society; and I believe that our modern blindness to the reality of this contract, and to the sobriety of Burke's phrases, has mightily impeded any alleviation of our present discontents, our maladies of spirit and of body politic. What Burke illuminates here is the necessity to any high and just civilization of a conscious belief in the value of continuity: continuity in religious and ethical conviction, continuity in literature and schooling, continuity in political and economic affairs, continuity in the physical fabric of life. I think we have neglected the principle of continuity to our present grave peril, so that with us, as Aristophanes said of his own generation, "Whirl is king, having overthrown

[3] John H. Hallowell: *Main Currents in Modern Political Thought,* p. 196. New York: Henry Holt, 1959.

Zeus." Men who do not look backward to their ancestors, Burke remarks elsewhere, will not look forward to their posterity.

If we retain any degree of concern for the future of our race, we need urgently to re-examine the idea of an eternal contract that joins the dead, the living, and those yet unborn. Even if we have lost most of that solicitude for posterity, still we may need to return to the principle of continuity out of simple anxiety for self-perservation.[4]

In a talk at Pepperdine College, Kirk saw Christianity as an aspect of Western tradition, and the foundation of civilization was for him tradition and continuity.[5] This for Kirk is the essence of truth, continuity. His application of Burke's concept is rigid in a way that Burke's was not. Burke retained as basic to tradition, however much he weakened that foundation, the absolute and sovereign God. For Kirk, this God is apparently totally a part of tradition and continuity. Burke favored the American colonists in the War of Independence; Kirk has made it clear that he would have been a Tory. Kirk has joined the Roman Catholic Church, but his writings give no evidence of either a Scholastic or Augustinian philosophy: he is still a believer in continuity and tradition. Is his "conversion" to Rome simply an adoption of a powerful tradition? In terms of his perspective, Kirk would not only have been a Tory in 1776, he would, if he were in the U.S.S.R. in 1966, be an old line Stalinist, and, in A.D. 20, he would have, in the name of "the principle of continuity," joined the Sanhedrin in crucifying Christ. who openly denounced tradition in the name of truth.

A deadly use of Burkean continuity was made by Harold O. Rugg, the educator, whose textbooks eloquently portrayed

[4] Russell Kirk: *A Program for Conservatives*, p. 197. Chicago: Regnery, 1954.
[5] Russell Kirk: *Pepperdine College Forum V*, "Roots of Our Civilization." n.d. (1962?).

the American tradition as radicalism, as a long resistance to federalism and constitutionalism in the name of social democracy. Rugg could point to the 20th century American development as evidence that the true tradition and vital continuity is on the left, so that Kirk's Tory faith is a hot-house plant by comparison.[6]

[6] Gary North in a review in The Riverside, California, Sunday Press Enterprise "Diversion," January 2, 1966, p. E-11, wrote of Kirk's The Intemperate Professor:

The late Whittaker Chambers once remarked that he could not imagine American boys dying for Russell Kirk's brand of conservatism. Kirk's latest book would not have changed his opinion.

The theme of the book is one of Kirk's favorites: Americans do not read enough Cicero. With the decline of "humane letters" has come the decline of the American republic. Americans, unwilling to read a serious book, have become afflicted with the worst disease of all: bad taste.

His chapters on the inconsistencies of liberals in the academic community are, as always, amusing. The important chapters, however, deal with religion and morals. They are important not for what they reveal about America, but for what they reveal of Kirk.

The spiritual emptiness of modern man, he argues, can be cured only by a "genuine restoration of the higher religious understanding, of transcendent truth, of the sense of the numinous." The Heisenberg principle of indeterminancy has brought modern science back to an appreciation of the universe's mystery, so why not the churches?

This is not conservatism; it is modern secular irrationalism. Kirk correctly diagnoses the theological error in modern American religion: Pelagianism. But he is not about to return to the Augustinian answer to Pelagius. Instead of a return to trinitarian orthodoxy, we need to accept some form of the "New Reformation" theology, the theological system made famous by Karl Barth of Switzerland.

Kirk seems blissfully unaware of the voluminous writings of Professor Cornelius Van Til of Westminster Seminary. Van Til has shown clearly the incompatibility of Barth's neo-orthodoxy with the Reformation faith to which Kirk gives lip service.

Kirk's theology, as he demonstrates in this book, is a curious mixture of the Niebuhrs, Barth, Robert Fitch, Tillich, and just enough Billy Graham to placate the evangelicals. He sees in the modern ecumenical church movement the hope for the conservative future.

Whatever one's opinion about these modern theological movements, it seems safe to say that they are not in the mainstream of conservative American Christianity. In proclaiming them in the name of conservatism, Kirk demonstrates that he, like so many

Truth as continuity and tradition, as roots, is a deadly concept. What if a man's "roots" be cannibalism, Islam, Buddhism, Hinduism, or animism? Is he obligated to remain in that tradition and to receive new insights only in terms of his brand of "the great primaeval contract of eternal society"? This philosophy has all the fertility of a mule, and its social dynamics reaches from the professor's podium to the second row of seats. It is a great faith for little men.

A *third* concept of truth, one very widely prevalent, is the concept of *truth as factuality*. This faith has been very succinctly stated by Lenny Bruce: "Truth is 'what is.' " [7] In terms of this faith, everything which exists or occurs in nature is thereby both natural and is the truth concerning reality. The thinking of Kinsey rested on this premise. For him, any form of sexual activity, whether homosexuality, animal contacts, or anything else, was equally normal and true as normal marital relations because it was equally "natural," i.e., existent in nature. [8]

Truth as factuality is a concept with a long history,

of the "National Review" staff, is a conservative on certain issues, but that in the area of first principles he stands on the same philosophical foundation as does the modern liberal.

American Society is said to be saved by a return to classical studies and a belief in "the numinous." This mediocre little volume, in short, represents a return to gnosticism; its faith is in an unnamed mystery, frightening, and hardly a comfort to mankind. Man is left in fear and trembling, with a paperback copy of the Iliad to protect him.

Chambers was right; this type of conservatism is not worth dying for.

[7] Lenny Bruce, "How to talk dirty and influence people," *Playboy*, vol. II, no. 1, January, 1964, p. 182.

[8] See Edmund Bergler, M.D.: *Counterfeit-Sex: Homosexuality, Impotence, Frigidity*, pp. viii-x, for comments on Freud; New York: Grune and Stalton, 1958, second edition, enlarged. For Kinsey's defense of child-molestation, see Alfred C. Kinsey, Wardell B. Pomeroy, Clyde E. Martin, Paul Gebbard, etc.: *Sexual Behavior in the Human Female*, pp. 115, 121f., 327f., 330; Philadelphia: W. B. Saunders, 1953.

and it has been associated with Cynicism, nihilism, anarchism, and with socialism. It is closely linked with the student radicalism of the 1960's. In every age, its function is negative and destructive. It acts as a corrosive and hostile force against civilization but is itself totally sterile and incapable of any act of reconstruction. Because truth is everything except that which is exclusive, apart from destroying law and order, this faith simply accepts the status quo of evil. This is its ultimate implication and always its mediate purpose, even when unacknowledged.

A *fourth* concept of truth is a *pragmatic* approach, one in which truth is seen as beyond good and evil, and beyond the normal sense of contradiction between truth and untruth. Friedrich Nietzsche stated this position more clearly and honestly than many of his followers:

> The falseness of an opinion is not for us any objection to it: it is here, perhaps, that our new language sounds most strangely. The question is, how far an opinion is life-furthering, life-preserving, perhaps species-rearing; and we are fundamentally inclined to maintain that the falsest opinions (to which the synthetic judgments *a priori* belong), are the most indispensable to us: that without a recognition of logical fictions, without a comparison of reality with the purely *imagined* world of the absolute and immutable, without a constant counterfeiting of the world by means of numbers, man could not live—that the renunciation of false opinions would be a renunciation of life, a negation of life. *To recognize untruth as a condition of life:* that is certainly to impugn the traditional ideas of value in a dangerous manner, and a philosophy which ventures to do so, has thereby alone placed itself beyond good and evil.[9]

Levi has aptly described Nietzsche's position as "at least in part the assertion of a will to illusion."[10] The Freudian,

[9] *The Philosophy of Nietzsche*, "Beyond Good and Evil," p. 4, Ch. I, 4. New York: The Modern Library.
[10] Albert William Levi: *Philosophy and the Modern World*, p. 40. Bloomington: Indiana University Press, 1959.

Otto Rank, stated that "With the truth one cannot live. To be able to live one needs illusions." [11]

This will to illusion has been formalized into a variety of philosophies, pragmatism, instrumentalism, existentialism, logical analysis, and others. These philosophies reduce truth to what works, to the successful illusion, to the powerful lie. Neo-orthodoxy shows very clearly the influences of this position. By placing truth beyond good and evil, beyond normal standards of truth and untruth, this philosophy in actuality denies the validity of truth as truth and substitutes for it, as its mainspring and foundational principle, *power*. Instead of truth, it moves in terms of power, and, as a result, the followers of this faith today, whether in the church or in the academy, gravitate to politics and to power. The world of politics is for them *the real world* because it is for them *the world of power*, their only truth.

As against all these and other positions, a *fifth* position is that of Biblical Christianity. Truth is a Person, Jesus Christ, the second Person of the Trinity, and truth is His infallible and enscriptured word. Jesus declared, "I am the way, the truth, and the life: no man cometh unto the Father, but by me" (John 14:6). Since "All things were made by him, and without him was not any thing made that was made" (John 1:3), all things are only truly understandable in terms of Him and His creative purpose. The true interpretation of reality is possible only in terms of the triune God, of whom Jesus Christ is the declaration or exegesis (John 1:18: he hath declared him or *exegesato,* has made known). Apart from Him, the universe quickly falls apart, in human thought, into a world of illusion or of brute factuality, with every fact unrelated to all others. The denial of the triune God is the denial ultimately of meaning, community, nature, family, life, culture, and of

[11] *Ibid.*, p. 186.

all things, and the collapse of man's existence into hell, total unrelatedness and meaninglessness. Only by left-handed and partial affirmations of God's eternal decree have cultures apart from Christianity been able to exist. The growing epistemological self-consciousness of man is increasingly pushing for a total war against God and therefore against culture and civilization.

Jesus Christ, by His hostility to the tradition of the rabbis, came as the destroyer of tradition and continuity in the name of truth. As the logos, He came as the destroyer of autonomous reason, of rationalism, in the name and as the visible incarnation of true wisdom. Because the ontological Trinity is the Creator of all things, the Trinity has priority in all categories of thought, for there neither can be nor is there law, society, justice, structure, design or meaning apart from God. The denial of God is therefore the denial of truth, life, relationships, values, society, science, art, and all things else. The nihilistic and anarchistic course of man as he denies the triune God is an inescapable consequence of man's departure from God. The ground of historical action is the governing conception of truth of an era or group, and, as man turns his back on the truth, Jesus Christ, his historical action is increasingly nihilistic and anarchistic.

VIII

INESCAPABLE KNOWLEDGE

One of the fundamental premises of the Bible is that the knowledge of God is both inescapable and universal. Repeatedly the Scripture asserts the universal nature of the witness of all creation to God (Psalm 19:1-4), and Paul asserted that God's wrath against all ungodliness was based on this universal and inescapable knowledge:

> For the wrath of God is revealed from heaven against all ungodliness and unrighteousness of men, who hold the truth in unrighteousness; Because that which may be known of God is manifest in them; for God hath shewed it unto them. For the invisible things of him from the creation of the world are clearly seen, being understood by the things that are made, even his eternal power and Godhead: so that they are without excuse (Rom. 1:18-20).

As is well known by Biblical scholars, the word "hold" can be better rendered as "hold down" or "suppress," i.e., men "hold down (or suppress) the truth in unrighteousness." Men drive this inescapable knowledge of God out of their consciousness into their unconscious because it is a knowledge that militates against their own desire to be as gods (Gen. 3:5).

A corollary of this premise of inescapable knowledge is the fact that men will consciously know God either by faith or by judgment. In one way or another, God will be known by *all* men. In Ezekiel, this inescapable knowledge by judgment is repeatedly stressed: "And they shall know that I am

74

the LORD, and that I have not said in vain that I would do this evil unto them" (Ez. 6:10). This statement, with minor variations, is made 72 times in Ezekiel. It is present, moreover, in all of Scripture in varying forms.

An important aspect of history, therefore, and of any Biblical philosophy of history, is inescapable knowledge in the form of judgment. This concept when broadly stated, i.e., the concept of inescapable knowledge in the form of judgment, finds acceptance in varying philosophies. Marxism, for example, is confident that the course of history will bring judgment on capitalism and force even the capitalists to recognize that history is against them. More than a few philosophies hold that historical process will vindicate their truth, and they thus are ready to assert a form of knowledge by judgment.

But it is one thing to affirm the inexorable judgment of historical process; it is another to hold to the personal judgment of the personal and triune God. More than one person has cited the famous line from the Song of Deborah, "The stars in their courses fought against Sisera" (Judges 5:20), but with varying meanings. To cite a few, *first*, for some, it means that historical process militates against tyranny and tyrants. *Second*, for others, it means that the human spirit continually rises against tyranny, and it is the essence of man to seek freedom. *Third*, for the Christian, it means that the triune God who created all things has destined all things to serve Him, and all creation serves His personal will and therefore wars against His enemies. These three views have a superficial resemblance in that they see purpose in history, but they have an actual hostility to one another. The personalism of the Biblical view is an offense to other faiths. Men are ready to believe that history and the universe are purposeless and mindless, and that disasters, deaths, earthquakes, and plagues are unrelated to any mind or will. The idea that a mind could be behind these events they find offensive. Why? The reason commonly cited through the centuries is that it is offensive to believe that a supreme mind and power, God, could permit such catastrophes or show such heartless wrath. Better a mindless disaster than a mindful one. This position, of course, insists that events it does not like are inescapably wrong for God to indulge in, a major assumption and a thoroughly anthropocentric one.

But an even more basic issue underlies the objection. *First,* by removing God from the universe and making history impersonal, *morality* is removed from history and *process* replaces it. By this simple act man transfers himself, in his thinking, *from a sinner to a victim.* The result is a tremendous "advance" for humanistic man. It removes him from the criminal's bench and puts him in the role of plaintiff. In the role of criminal, of sinner, man is the object of God's judgment and legal action. In the role of plaintiff, man is the party who begins an action at law. Man thereby makes of himself an accuser of any God who may appear on the scene against him.

Second, by removing God from the universe, man gives priority to himself and his own purposes. The universe and history, instead of being under the sovereign purposes of the triune God, are instead open to the attempt of scientific, humanistic man to impose his will and purpose upon them. Man becomes thereby his own god and sovereign. It is to man's advantage therefore to ridicule the concept of a personal God expressing His wrath and judgment in history. A mindless universe is preferred, because it can beget a man-god to govern that "open" universe.

The objection, then, is not on intellectual grounds: it is on immoral grounds. Men, in St. Paul's phrase, hold down or suppress the truth in unrighteousness, and the objections to judgment in history by the personal and triune God are a manifestation of that suppressing drive which runs deeper

76

than book-burning: its goal is the obliteration of a world of thought.

Ezekiel specified, among the forms of judgment, famine, pestilence, and sword (Ez. 6:11-14). With Elijah, it was a three and a half year total drought (I Kings 17:1, James 5:17f). Isaiah and Zechariah cited earthquakes as means of judgment (Isa. 29:6; Zech. 14:5; cf. Rev. 6:12; 8:5; 11:13, 19; 16:18). The catalogue of Deuteronomy 28 is even more extensive and specific.

This does not mean that all disasters are to be read in terms of man, or in terms of judgment upon man. Such a reading of history, very prevalent in 18th century Deism, is anthropocentric.[1] The world of man and nature moves, not in terms of man but God. Jesus attacked this man-centered reading of events (Luke 13:1-5). The point of reference is God, not man; the prior realm is eternity, not time. The doctrine of poetic justice is a man-centered reading of history and an insistence that the concerns of time have priority over history, and, therefore, full justice must be rendered in time. Poetic justice calls for the due rewarding and the due punishing of men in history. It is a doctrine of the Enlightenment and of its early optimism. Thomas Rymer (1678) gave poetic justice its formal name, and it is significant that Rymer was greatly influenced by Leibnitz. In its *first* form, Deism, Enlightenment optimism held to poetic (or poetical) justice, the rewarding of all men in time by the law of Nature. In its *second* form, Enlightenment optimism, disillusioned by Nature, turned to man and held to a new form of poetic justice, Socialism. Under Socialism, poetic justice is expected to prevail: all men will be given their due and perfect reward or punishment in time. *Socialism is thus the modern form of the doctrine of poetic justice.* It is an intellectual absurdity and

[1] See T. D. Kendrick: *The Lisbon Earthquake.* Philadelphia: J. B. Lippencott, 1956.

a concept that can lead only to disillusionment.

Concepts of justice vary markedly, and the justice of one system is injustice to another faith. But in virtually all systems there is a demand for justice, a hunger for the total righting of all ills, and the restitution of all things. Man seeks the perfect social order, but his search has a double halter on it. *First*, man the sinner wants a just world and perfect righteousness without the necessity of repentance and regeneration on his part. Every man wants a perfect and a completely faithful wife, but not every man is ready to be a godly and faithful husband. The expectation of justice and perfection is imposed upon the social order: it is not required of one's self. Thus, the demand for justice by the sinner is in essence for a world in which his sin will not receive its due reward, or punishment, but will instead be nullified by the prevailing perfection.

Second, justice, absolute, final and perfect justice can be sought in time or in eternity. The search for perfect and final justice in time is the Enlightenment doctrine of poetic justice; it is Socialism. If the locale and source of perfect justice is God and eternity, then heaven and hell provide the answer, and God's judgments in history are partial manifestations of a forthcoming and total justice. The humanistic dream of justice, the dream of autonomous reason, is purely of this world. Perfect justice must be realized in this world, and its source is the scientific socialist state and its social engineers. The locale of heaven and hell is therefore in this world, and the "just social order" seeks to create a heaven on earth while abolishing the social reprobates to hell. It must be noted that socialism has been markedly successful in half its goal: it creates a hell on earth very easily, but it has failed to give man anything remotely resembling a heaven on earth. But heaven and hell are inescapable categories of human existence. Men

78

will either acknowledge their role in terms of eternity or seek to create them in time, with devastating results.

God's judgments in history are personal and real, but they are not total judgment or total justice. Such an expectation belongs to the end of history and to eternity. But the judgments are nonetheless real. It is interesting to note the escalation in disasters since 1950, as compared to the first half of the century. The following data, from an Almanac compilation into the latter part of 1963, are of interest:

Major earthquakes and volcanic eruptions:
1900–1949   8 major occurrences in the world
1950–1963   10 major occurrences in the world

Major floods, avalanches, and tidal waves:
1900–1949   8 major occurrences in the world
1950–1963   12 major occurrences in the world

Man-killing, building levelling hurricanes:
1900–1949   17 major occurrences in the world
1950–1963   19 major occurrences in the world

It has also been noted that, since World War II, there are "fewer thunderstorms around the world, and thus less rainfall in selected areas. There also seems to be a sharp decline in natural nitrogen fertilizers, since soil nitrogen is largely produced by lightning and reaches earth in the rainfall that accompanies thunderstorms." [2]

To believe that these events can be an aspect of God's justice and judgment is a matter of faith. To one who denies the sovereign and triune God, it is absurd to see God's hand in natural events, or in any events. Justice for the humanist is a matter of social action. But, it must be insisted that it is no less a matter of faith to hold that these snivelling and sordid socialists and scientific planners

---

[2] Peter Lamb, "The Bomb Has Changed the Weather," in *Saga*, p. 59, vol. 32, no. 2, May, 1966. The title indicates the thesis of this article.

are capable of ushering in the reign of justice than it is to believe that God judges man by earthquakes and disasters. On the contrary, it takes a far greater faith to believe that these socialistic politicians and scientists, with their staggering self-righteousness, their sniggling evil, and their whining complaint that all their errors are due to someone else, can ever produce justice than it does to believe that the God revealed by Scripture shall bring it to pass. The great and credulous believers of the 20th century are the socialists.

But even these "true believers" will be brought to the inescapable knowledge of God, if not by faith then by judgment.

When Israel defiled nature in its apostasy, then God gave nature a rest by depopulating Israel through war, captivity, plague, and famine. Seventy years' rest was promised the land by God (II Chron. 87:21; Jer. 29:10). God had cursed the earth with man's fall (Gen. 3:17), and again with the Flood, but, after the Flood, God declared that He would no more curse the earth for man's sake (Gen. 8:20-22). The earth will not share further, on any large scale, in man's sin. It groans and travails waiting for the glorious consummation at the end of all things (Rom. 8:22, 23), and, before then, the triumph of Christ's Kingdom in time (Isa. 65:20-25). In the words of Isaiah 11:9, and also of Hab. 2:14, "The earth shall be full of the knowledge of the LORD, as the waters cover the sea." The goal of history is the inescapable knowledge of God.

In the procession of history to that end, Ezekiel 6:6 declares, men's works apart from God will be abolished, or blotted out. Either our sins are blotted out by the blood of Christ, or our works are blotted out by the judgment of God. And the works of socialism and statism in every form are destined to be abolished and blotted out.

But to discuss judgment is to run counter to the spirit of the age. As McNeile Dixon observed,

> The kind-hearted humanitarians of the nineteenth century decided to improve on Christianity. The thought of hell offended their susceptibilities. They closed it, and to their surprise the gates of Heaven closed also with a melancholy bang. The malignant countenance of Satan disturbed them. They dispensed with him and at the same time God took His departure.[3]

Judgment, however, is inescapable. We cannot save man from crime without punishing crime. Salvation requires judgment. Thus the hope of the faithful for salvation involves the expectation of judgment. Morris, in analyzing the Biblical doctrine of judgment, has called attention to the relationship between judgment and salvation, punishment and deliverance:

> The judge not only discovered what was right, but acted upon it. If all the evidence was not in he went out until he found what was missing, that justice, real justice, be done. Thus one and the same verb may mean 'to punish' or 'to deliver.'[4]

> The God of the New Testament does not sit back and let 'natural' law bring about the defeat of evil.[5]

Without judgment, there can be no salvation. The salvation of Noah from a world of tyranny was the judgment and destruction of that world by a Flood. The salvation of Israel from Egypt meant the judgment and destruction of Egypt. The Cross of Christ is the supreme coincidence of judgment and salvation. It is God's judgment and sentence of death on man the sinner, and also God's salvation through the atoning death of Jesus Christ.

We cannot accept salvation if we reject judgment. In

[3] Cited by Leon Morris: *The Biblical Doctrine of Judgment*, p. 69. Grand Rapids: Eerdmans, 1960.
[4] *Ibid.*, p. 17.
[5] *Ibid.*, p. 70.

order to save godly men from an evil and apostate generation, God must judge that generation and destroy its works, and the believer must move in terms of that reality. The reality is simply this: *no judgment, no salvation.* This means, moreover: *no judgment, no God.* Judgment reveals God and His justice. Justice makes for progress in history. Instead of an endless cycle of causality which shuts up men in a process, in a treadmill, in *Karma*, judgment frees men from their past and saves them from their history. The doctrine of *Karma* is a logical development of the concept of causality in history, and its conclusion is the despair of history. Man cannot escape his past, and his future is endlessly chained to an expiation of the past, to the mechanical outworkings of unrelenting causality. God's judgments in history may wipe out a people, but they can also deliver a people from their history and release them into a new hope for the future.

Those who hate judgment hate salvation also; they resent deliverance. Men who hate God's judgment want the total enslavement of man, his entrapment in guilt and in the outworkings of past history. If there be no judgment, no salvation is possible.

Judgment gives freedom. The Christian can "have boldness in the day of judgment" (I John 4:17), because he has already undergone judgment in the person and cross of Christ. The Lord's Prayer, "Thy kingdom come, *Thy will be done,*" is a prayer in part for judgment. And, as C. F. D. Moule pointed out, "both the sacraments involve a doctrine of judgment. Baptism is regarded as dying with Christ and rising with Him. . . . Baptism 'is essentially pleading guilty, accepting the verdict. . . .' Holy Communion should be preceded by self-knowledge, otherwise it will be followed by the divine judgment (I Cor. xi. 28f)." [6]

Judgment is thus not only an aspect of the inescapable

[6] Cited in *ibid.*, p. 56f.

knowledge of God: it is also a basic aspect of salvation. The personal judgment of God in history cannot be removed from history without removing God from history. And it cannot be done.

A NOTE ON SOCIALIST POETIC JUSTICE

The prize examples of poetic justice in literature are not the writings of the Enlightenment but in the literature of socialism. An amusing episode is narrated by Kyra Petrovskaya. A Georgian Communist in the U.S.S.R. was assigned to collectivize the Eskimos, who resisted because they failed to understand what it meant. After some effort, the Communist won the friendship of the Eskimo chief, who then demonstrated his friendship by ordering his wife to lie with the Communist.

You know, of course, that the Eskimos never wash, and the women also use fish oil on their hair, which adds one more bad smell to their already appalling odiferousness. However, our man knew that if he refused this highest of honors, his whole mission would be wasted. So, resigning himself, he lay down with the malodorous lady, hoping she wouldn't insist upon his fulfilling the conjugal obligation. The candle was blown out. He made no move toward her, and she remained at a proper distance—but just as the poor devil was beginning to relax, the candle flared again, the chief shuffled over to his pallet, and announced that he was very disappointed to have heard no sounds of sensual enjoyment thus far. The ceremony, he said, would be enacted immediately, before his eyes. . . . So the poor man closed his eyes, held his breath, and doubtlessly thinking, "The things I do for Stalin," somehow managed to get through the performance. . . .

Next day, the whole tribe, hearing that the chief had bestowed this greatest of accolades upon the intruder, signed up for the establishment of a *Kolkhoz*.

The missionary then began to build himself a house which

83

we helped him to finish, and shortly afterward his wife Nina arrived. She was a beautiful woman in her early thirties. We were all so delighted to see her that we gave a fine party in her honor. Everyone had a marvellous time and Nina seemed to enjoy herself hugely. However, the Eskimo chief remained after all the other guests had gone, and, to the Georgian's horror, spread out his blanket, announcing that he was ready to accept a return gesture of friendship from his host. Furthermore, the Georgian, after a few minutes struggle with his conscience, firmly demanded that Nina help him carry out his bargain of *noblesse oblige* with the chief.

. . . Now, if his wife refused to sleep with the chief, the meticulous work of many weeks would have gone for nought. The Eskimos would take offense, the *Kolkhoz* would fall apart, his mission would be a failure; and, as every good Communist knows, the Party never forgives a failure. So, this Georgian's future, perhaps even his life, depended on his wife's understanding and cooperation. Unfortunately, however, Nina, who wasn't a Party member, felt no overwhelming sense of duty toward it. When the chief's request was translated to her, and her husband commanded that she comply with it, she screamed and ran out of his house. She came to me for refuge and stayed overnight in my little hut. Next morning she left camp. . . . All the poor missionary's plans promptly went awry, he was called back to Moscow, and, of course, we never heard from him again.

This incident was later made into a play called Oorka, *The White Wolf*. But the play gave an ending in conformity to the demand for Socialist Justice:

Well, in the play, the wife agrees to sacrifice herself for the sake of the new *Kolkhoz*. But at the last minute she is saved by the chief himself, who suddenly realizes the barbarity of his tribal custom and reforms completely.[1]

The play thus, if not reality, met all the demands of socialist poetic justice. The Communist organizer did his

[1] Kyra Petrovskaya: *Kyra*, p. 138ff. Englewood Cliffs, New Jersey: Prentice-Hall, April, 1959.

duty, and the wife did her's, and the result was a *Socialist ex machina* salvation.

This demand for poetic justice is imposed on historiography also by socialism. Periodically, Communist history books are rewritten to eliminate certain episodes from history and introduce fancied ones in order to meet the requirements of poetic justice. History must see a neat and perfect working of Socialist Justice *in time*, but regrettably for the socialists, while fortunately for mankind, this Socialist Justice works out only in history books, not in history.

In Western countries, literature is also heavily infected by the doctrine of Socialist Justice. Capitalists are, in such writings, monsters headed for destruction, and the clergy are hypocritical, sensual parasites, Elmer Gantrys, and time brings retribution to them, physical or spiritual. "Socialist Realism" in writing is simply the socialist version of the Enlightenment doctrine of poetic justice.

Western historiography is increasingly an hagiographic narrative of the saints of socialism. It reeks with the moralisms of Socialist Justice. It is less and less history and more and more the formula of *1984*.

In its earlier form, poetic justice was seen as the workings of Nature. In its present form, it is increasingly seen as the product of the scientific socialist state, which, in Marxist thought, is the product of Nature destined to bring in full justice.

In the Biblical perspective, because the world is fallen and in sin, it moves in terms of injustice rather than justice. However, because God created the world and absolutely governs it, the world is being brought under the dominion of justice by the Kingship of Christ. The full realization of justice, however, is reserved to eternity.

Poetic justice, in its every form involves an acceptance of a status quo. In its earlier states, Nature was the substitute concept for God, and therefore the world of Nature was normative. It was held that this is the best of all possible worlds, and, as a result, the Enlightenment accepted the status quo except with respect to Christianity. Christianity as a supernatural and by implication anti-Natural (in the Deistic sense) Religion, had to be overthrown. Instead of a fallen world, Natural Religion held to a normative world. Instead of seeking to redeem and save a fallen world, Natural Religion accepted it as is.

In its present form, poetic justice still accepts the status quo, but this time it is the status quo of statism. It is hostile to Christianity, but agreeable to all else virtually. Lenny Bruce has said, "the religious leaders are 'what *should be.*' . . . Let me tell you the truth. The truth is 'what is.' If 'what is' is, you have to sleep eight, ten hours a day, that is the truth. A lie will be: people need no sleep at all. Truth is 'what is.'" [2] If "truth is 'what is,'" then acceptance of the truth is acceptance of the status quo and it is opposition to Christianity and its insistence on "*what should be.*" Progress becomes impossible in a world in which "what is" is normative.

[2] Lenny Bruce, *op. cit.*

IX

INCARNATION AND HISTORY

When men speak of religion, they commonly mean some kind of belief in God. In this definition, they reveal their Christian cultural background, because virtually all religions are non-theistic. There is no God in what is termed animism: merely impersonal forces or charges in things. Buddhism is an atheistic religion, relativistic and pessimistic in nature, and Jainism is mainly a worship of life, not of God. Confucianism, a philosophy become religion, is non-theistic, and the same is true of Taoism. Hinduism has many gods, but ultimate reality is not a personal God but ultimate process, and much the same is true of Shintoism. Despite the facade of Biblical borrowings, Mohammedanism is basically a religion of impersonalism. Significantly, in Islam it is not a church representing a transcendental order which is the primary institution, but the state, a present order, an immanent power. The mosque is under the state and a branch of the state. As a Moslem writer has noted of Islam, "its adaptability to progress and government power is incomparable. It has always been in the service of the State." [1] Apart from Biblical faith, there is no truly theistic religion, and Biblical religion is unique in its affirmation of a totally personal and sovereign God.

Because in other religions either a universe is in process, or a totally immanent (but non-personal) divinity is resi-

[1] Youssef El Masry: *Daughters of Sin: The Sexual Tragedy of Arab Women*, p. 34. New York: Macfadden, 1963.

dent in history, the state is the decisive and total order of man. The state either represents the high point and incarnation of process, or it is the incarnation of the resident divinity of being, in that the state is the locale of power in history. The state has the power of the sword: it can kill man or confiscate man's wealth. The state is power, and, in an atheistic world, power is the only god men recognize and therefore obey. If there be no God beyond man, then the state becomes the god for men as the supreme power over men.

The goal of history in non-Christian systems usually falls into one of two categories. *First,* some systems see the material world as something to be transcended, something to be outgrown, so that man, born into this world, must seek to escape this world. The evolution of being is towards an escape from its womb of matter into the freedom of spirit. Such world and life views are non-theistic and they are pessimistic with respect to man, matter, and consciousness. *Second,* other systems reject this escape from matter and history into spirit, from the world of material necessity into the world of free spirit. For these systems, the material world is the *given,* and the goal of history is to incarnate in this material world a new element struggling up out of this world; this new element is the mind, purpose, and goal of man. The world, in this perspective, moves from the kingdom of necessity to the realm of freedom as the will of the people is incarnated in a social order dedicated to a total mastery of nature as the means of man's freedom.

In the first position, the state commands history by default. No other power is real, and, although power is an aspect of the lower and evolving world of being, it is the only power that commands and hence reigns. Despotism is thus the natural conequence. In the second position, statism is not simply a consequence of this philosophy but its chosen and holy purpose and goal. In either case, man is supposedly to find freedom from the natural necessities of the material world. What man finds instead is the bondage of the omnipotent state. In either case, the meaning or *exegesis* of history is derived from man and man's reasoning. Meaning is derived from the creature. Man becomes his own Word: the Word is Man. Man is the reason and the power of the universe, and the form of man is the state because man is seen as a social and political animal.

But according to the Biblical faith, the meaning of history is not from history but beyond history. The meaning of history is the triune and sovereign God, and, according to John 1:18, "No man hath seen God at any time; the only begotten Son, which is in the bosom of the Father, he hath declared him." The word "declared" in the Greek original is "exegesato"; Jesus Christ is the exegesis, the declaration, the revelation of God. In Him the exegesis of God and of all God's purposes, including the meaning of history, is manifested. Because Christ is the *truth*, the exegesis of God, the primacy of history is with Him and in Him, and the truth of history. The state, the Great Society or Great Community, or the one-world order, is not the evolving and incarnating truth of history; Christ is the truth, by whom all things were made. He is the alpha and omega, the finality and totality of meaning.

But, because man is a sinner in rebellion against the truth, man is determined to create his own truth, his own image. Man's approach to the truth is thus anthropocentric and anti-Christian. In approaching the truth, the natural man takes a number of courses in trying to supplant Christ. Three common approaches are the following. *First*, Christ is made wholly man so that the door to divinity is left open to man. Christ is made man so that man might become God, in such thinking. In some earlier forms, the deity of Christ was acknowledged, but it was a divinity which was captured for all men. This is the *second* form of negation:

89

Christ's divinity is made the potential or actual divinity of all men. The only uniqueness of Christ in this view was that He was one of the first "masters" to capture divinity for men. *Third*, it is held that the state is the Word; the Great Society is "the Light, which lighteth every man" rather than Jesus Christ (John 1:9).

A *fourth* means whereby an attempt is made to supplant Christ is by means of "tradition." The essence of truth is not in the incarnate person of Jesus Christ and His finished and infallible word, the Scripture, but in a process. A developing, growing, often pluralistic process is a work in history, and the incarnation of meaning is to be found in this process. This process is called Jesus Christ. According to the World Council of Churches: "*The* Tradition is the history in and by which all Christians live," the history of Christ, and the history of the church, "the living history of all history, gathering up the history of Israel, centering in the history of Jesus Christ, and continuing in the history of the church, in *saecula saeculorum. The* Tradition is also the history of the future since its final goal is Christ's victory over all 'dominions, authorities and powers'—and the consummation of all things (I Cor. 15:24-26) . . . the Lordship of Christ over history is exercised through his participation in it." This means that Christ can rule history *only* by participation in it. In other words, the lordship of Christ is in His humanity, not in His deity, because the determination of history is in time, not in eternity. *The* Tradition is "pluralistic," and "none of the plural traditions has the intrinsic authority to disinherit the others. All have a basic right to be considered and appraised in the light of their professed intention to be obedient to *the* Tradition." [2] The test of

[2] Paul S. Minear, editor: *Faith and Order Findings, The Final Report of the Theological Commission to the Fourth World Conference on Faith and Order*, Montreal, 1963, "The Renewal of the Christian Tradition," The Report of the North American Section, Albert C. Outler, Chairman, p. 18f. Minneapolis: Augsburg, 1963.

authenticity is thus not an infallible word of supernatural authority but the "professed intention to be obedient to *the* Tradition." Thus, as this growing Tradition incorporates various religious traditions, the professed intention of each to be faithful to the growing process will make them equally "Christian."

Room is made for this to happen: "we have found ourselves in unforced agreement that no *doctrine* of tradition, or of 'Scripture and tradition,' can be adequate unless it is informed and reformed by a critical sense of history." This "critical sense of history" is not an evolution of the meaning of historical events but rather an existential absorption with the meaning of the moment. The critical and decisive meaning of history is thus not in Scripture nor in any *historical* tradition but in the existential history of the tradition:

> What we mean by a 'characteristically *historical* interpretation' of human events is not a *casual* explanation, nor the enunciation of a general theory about the meaning of history. Rather, we have in mind that sort of insight which arises in a decisive 'moment' of meaningful retrospect and prospect, which alters a man's appraisal of the Christian past and enlarges his freedom toward the Christian future. Such an experience, in its turn, illuminates the cognate question of the quality and meaning of human existence which, being radically historical, requires historical perspective for self-understanding.[3]

The new world order must have a catholic and ecumenical tradition which is sufficiently universal to include all men in their present faiths, however contradictory the one may be to another. In each and every one, the ecumenical, unitive *process* is at work. Stowe has given us a picture of this "future":

> Personally, I do not believe that a fruitful and humane world order can ever be expected on any basis other than

[3] *Ibid.*, p. 23.

91

the one identified in Acts 17: That God is building a unified world out of the treasures of all cultures and He is building it on the standard for human life which we see in Jesus.

If this is true we must have a vastly enlarged understanding of ecumenicity. Our horizon for spiritual questing and theological probing will not be the church alone, but the great issues and options generated by non-Christian norms for human life. We must listen with acute alertness to what is being said and why, when an Indonesian leader explains a massacre by saying "We are Moslems; we do not turn the other cheek." Or to a buddhist when he says that "Non-being or nothingness is . . . the ultimate principle." [4]

In such a perspective, room is made for all men, but not for the Jesus Christ of Scripture and history. *The exclusiveness of Jesus Christ is replaced by the inclusiveness of humanism.* All exclusiveness is thus seen as anti-humanistic, and increasingly legislative and administrative efforts are directed against exclusiveness, against any faith which distinguishes between men. All evil is seen as caused by exclusiveness, and the epitome of evil is seen as the God of Scripture, the God Who by his eternal decree elects some to salvation and others to reprobation. Accordingly, the politics of humanism is dedicated to total inclusion of all peoples, the criminal included, save those who are in any degree exclusive in their faith: these constitute the new criminal class. At one Job Corps Camp in the United States, the philosophy of the camp, according to a former counsellor, is "spoil these boys—they have never been spoiled before." The result there, as elsewhere, was lawlessness. Gang rapes, drunkenness, extortion, and other offenses were commonplace.

[4] Dr. David Metz Stowe, "Two Centuries—One Mission," Commencement Address, Pacific School of Religion, *Pacific School of Religion Bulletin*, vol. XLV, no. 2, June, 1966, p. 4.

Trainees have been arrested on charges ranging from sodomy, to assault, to drunkenness. Recently 30 members were invited to an evening's entertainment at the town's auto raceway. The job corpsmen showed their appreciation by shouting obscenities and creating a small scale riot. Christopher Weeks, then Deputy Job Corps Director in Washington, explained away the "incident" *by blaming the citizens of Atterbury*:

"Many job corpsmen feel they are not welcome in the communities adjacent to Atterbury. . . . if they are rejected, they react accordingly—and who can blame them?" [5]

Clearly, in terms of the philosophy of humanism, we cannot blame the criminal: we must blame the victim. This philosophy is now world-wide; it is a part of U. S. foreign policy, and it is a part of the expectation of the various nations of the world, who regard their profligacy and poverty as a sign of virtue, and the prosperity of the U. S. as a sign of criminality. As a result, the demands made by these nations presuppose a duty on the part of the U. S. to provide for their every need in order to "atone" for the offense of American character and wealth. It is held that such nations have a "right" to American funds. As one American newspaper editorial noted:

The United States has passed foreign aid around so freely and to so many countries it shouldn't be surprising that many nations have come to look upon U. S. aid as a "right." But the utter arrogance of Chile's demands the other day ought to provide the final push for the long-proposed overhaul of these giveaway programs.

At the Organization of American States meeting in Rio de Janeiro, Chile proposed that this country guarantee financial aid to each Latin-American nation with no strings attached. Chile also proposed that basic Latin

[5] Patty Newman, Joyce Wenger: *Pass the Poverty Please!*, p. 98f. Whittier, California: Constructive Action, 1966.

93

products such as sugar, coffee, fruit and beef be given preferential treatment in U. S. and world markets.

To add insult to this suggestion, these demands were coupled with an attack by Chile's foreign minister. He accused the United States of using the OAS to strengthen its own security at the expense of Latin-American development.[6]

Not surprisingly, the American Negro demanded a like program, with Floyd McKissick, director of CORE (Congress of Racial Equality) proposing federal spending of "no less than 23 billion dollars a year for the next five years on the elevation of Negroes." The demand was made at a White House Conference on civil rights, June 1 and 2, 1966, in Washington, D. C. "There were frequent warnings of violence." A 30-member council composed of leaders in business, labor, education and civil rights went further, than McKissick: 70 billions a year in aid were proposed, for free education, guaranteed income, rent subsidies, new housing, and the like.[7]

In asking for these welfare subsidies, the Negroes are, it must be noted, asking for slavery, for welfarism is a form of slavery, and slavery is a form of welfarism. Welfarism is used to enslave peoples, and to break down the independence of the middle classes by confiscatory taxation. Not surprisingly, federal officials have urged minority groups to " 'take to the streets' to secure their 'rights' for its people." Militant action and civil disobedience, other names for violence, have been urged on Mexican-American and others[8]

In the "culture" of humanism, excellence must be de-

[6] "Chile's Insulting Demands," Oakland, California, *Tribune*, Wednesday, November 24, 1965.

[7] "Civil Rights: Can Any Program Satisfy Everyone?," in *U. S. News & World Report*, June 13, 1966, vol. LX, no. 24, pp. 60-62.

[8] "Federal Rights Officials Favor Civil Disobedience," in Los Angeles, *The Freedom Press*, vol. VI, no. 11, June 17, 1966, pp. 1, 3.

stroyed to make way for the equality of degradation and failure. And, for humanists, there is no culture unless it be humanistic. Thus William E. Schlosser, Ph.D., drama professor at Valley State College in the California San Fernando Valley, has said that "a cultural or humanistic attitude is acquired only by seeking out other people—by exchanging ideas." For Dr. Schlosser, culture "is primarily a humanistic state of mind." [9] In other words, for Dr. Schlosser a Christian "state of mind" is obviously uncultured; only those with his "humanistic state of mind" are cultured! He is the "Greek"; all others are barbarians!

But, according to anthropology, culture is the trait complex manifested by a tribe or a unit of mankind. As Henry R. Van Til pointed out, in *The Calvinistic Concept of Culture*, culture is religion externalized. Thus, culture is not a neutral enterprise; it is not simply basket-weaving, drama, and other such manifestations of human activity. Culture, wherever it is manifested, is the expression of the basic perspectives and commitments of a people, and it finds expression, not merely in the "arts," but in the totality of their life. Schlosser demanded a center for performing arts as evidence of culture; his demand is rather an expression of pseudo-culture; of an identification of culture with certain aspects of it. It is thus held that culture only exists as these highly professional entertainment media are taken seriously. Because certain aspects of Greek culture came to focus in drama, and the English Renaissance in Elizabethan drama, Schlosser sees the presence of the Stage as evidence of culture! But the modern drama is a witness to anti-culture and pseudo-culture, because, whenever it is serious, it is so melodramatically and pompously serious. It says in effect, "Go to now: we will create culture." Instead, it produces pretentious nonsense which increasingly speaks

[9] Mary Reinholz, "Professor Hits Cultural Lack," Woodland Hills, California, *Herald Tribune*, Sunday, June 12, 1966, p. 1.

only to an audience of Cultural Pretenders, people who confuse culture with a form.

The Schlossers of history are peripheral and insignificant, nor do they represent the major thrust of humanism. The purpose of humanism is to negate the "duality" of Biblical faith. Biblical religion presents man with two worlds, the perfect and eternal order, and the fallen, sinful order of time. The fallen world of time must be redeemed by God in Christ and conformed to the eternal order and to Jesus Christ, creation's sovereign. The goal of anti-Christian philosophy has been to overcome this duality, to reduce reality to one order, the order of time and man. Its purpose therefore is to abolish all transcendental meaning and reduce history and meaning to man, to remove the revelation and incarnation of Jesus Christ, the Second Person of the Trinity, and replace Him with the incarnation of man as the meaning of history. When history fully and totally expresses man only, then its only meaning is existential man, and history is the incarnation of the meaning of man. Halle's analysis of Hegel is relevant:

> (Man is God become partial.) History is the process by which God, having alienated himself in external objects, progressively overcomes his alienation by acquiring knowledge of the external objects, thereby making them a part of his subjective self again. Since man is real only in his identification with the Absolute (God), this means that: the world of which man is conscious as being external to himself, as being an objective world, represents his own alienated self (God's alienated self); by the process of coming to know it he makes it no longer alien, he comprehends it, he reincorporates it in himself; and this process goes on until there is no longer a dual world of subject and object, until the entire world has been comprehended, has been overcome and absorbed, until all being is finally one—the universal God who is indistinguishable from the human self; until all being is, more precisely, the Logos, for Hegel identified being in its totality with the rational.

History, for Hegel, is the dialectical process by which God overcomes his alienation. Replace "God" with "Man" and this is what history is for Marx as well.[10]

This step, taken logically by Marx in terms of Hegelianism, has since been taken by existentialism, Fabianism, pragmatism, and other forms of humanism. In terms of this, the answer to the question, "Does Man's Existence Have a Meaning?," is that man's existence can only have a meaning derived from man himself.[11]

Humanism thus concludes with the ultimacy of man. There is neither God nor law above, over, and beyond man. Man is his own law and god. For the *consistent* humanists, this means that there can be no law governing any action of man which is free and unforced, voluntary and self-ordained. As the University of California at Los Angeles student group, Bruins for Voluntary Parenthood and Sexual Liberty, stated in a 1966 mimeographed circular:

The United States of America is NOT part of the free world.

The United States of America is part of the ANTI-COMMUNIST WORLD. What makes a country part of the free world?

It is this: In a country which is part of the free world every activity and every act which involves no victim is a CONSITUTIONALLY GUARANTEED RIGHT.

This is not the case in the United States of America.

It will be in a few years. It will be in a few years, that

[10] Louis J. Halle, "Marx's Religious Drama," in *Encounter*, vol. XXV, no. 4, October, 1965, p. 30.

[11] This question was the title of a symposium held February 18 through March 11, 1966, at Foothill College, Los Altos Hills, California. The speakers were Sidney Hook, Maurice Natanson, Michael Scriven, James L. Leach, and Lewis W. Spitz. The answers were predictable. The prospectus said, "All those with a curiosity about the meaning of man and the miracle of his existence are invited to attend these important lectures." Man is now his own god and his own miracle!

is, provided that those who want the United States of America to be part of the free world pay the heavy price of expanding our constitutionally guaranteed rights to include all act and activities which involve no victim.

Society has no interests other than those of its members. If no member of a society is a victim, that society is not a victim.

LIBERTY is that state of affairs in which every act which involves no victim is a CONSTITUTIONALLY GUARANTEED RIGHT.

And in what areas is liberty lacking in the United States of America?

In numerous acts and activities involving no victim. Primarily in the "social" aspects of daily living. In numerous instances of pursuit of happiness involving no victim.

More specifically: voluntary cunnilinctus, voluntary fellatio, voluntary common law marriage, voluntary use of contraception by teenagers, voluntary homogenital acts, voluntary abortion (to claim that voluntary abortion involves a victim is to confuse potential with what exists— a confusion which makes rape of nonpregnant women morally obligatory), voluntary use of marijuana under the restrictions that apply to alcohol; voluntary writing, publishing, sale, buying, reading, and ownership of "hard core" pornography and materials which appeal only to "prurient" tastes; voluntary discussion of all of the above without using the dozen or so banned English, nonderogratory use of the banned English words, nude bathing on free beaches (beaches where dress is optional), voluntary sexual activities involving financial reward, solicitation by homosexuals under the same limitations applied to solicitation by heterosexuals, noncurfew for women residents of dorms and sororities; etc.

Let there be LIBERTY.

For the consistent humanist, this is the only logical position. The *platonic and pragmatic* humanist, however, believes himself to be a philosopher-king and destined to conform all men to his own conception of true humanity. His humanism is accordingly totalitarian instead of anarchistic.

The *consistent* humanist has only one sin, force, violence against man. Thus, Dr. Timothy Leary reduces law in effect to "two new commandments": *first*, "thou shalt not alter the consciousness of thy fellowman by electrical or chemical means," and, *second*, "Thou shalt not prevent thy fellowman from changing his consciousness by electrical or chemical means." [12]

In any case, humanism, because it hates transcendence, has two basic drives: *first*, the destruction of Christian faith, and, *second*, the defense of a humanist status quo, a denial of and an end to progress. The humanistic triumph in any society, whether in old China, with its centuries of stagnation, in the 18th century Europe of the Enlightenment, or in the present socialist world, is also the triumph of inertia. Free social energy, under humanism, is replaced by the energy of the whip, the driving of man into grudging service by the agents of the state. Because meaning has been reduced to man, and man reduced to the state, or to anarchic inertia, the impetus of meaning is gone from humanistic man. The "duality" which constantly reminds man of the destiny to which he is called by God is replaced by the denial of any meaning to history apart from man himself. And man, with no meaning beyond himself, remains content with himself. There is no prod of any standard: he is his own standard. As a result, humanism is only effective as an agency of destruction. The incarnation of humanism into history is simply the triumph of slavery and stagnation.

---

[12] Dr. Timothy Leary, Ph.D., "The Politics and Ethics of Ecstasy," *Cavalier*, vol. 16, no. 157, July, 1966, p. 52. Speech delivered at Town Hall, New York City.

Nyack College Library

X

COMTE'S LAW AND HISTORY

Agnostic and atheistic historiography begins with a fundamental act of faith, the faith that God has nothing to do with history. This assumption has nothing to do with science or history: it is a pre-theoretical axiom with which all factuality is approached. Lucretius stated it openly and clearly: "The basic principle that we shall assume as our standing point is that nothing has ever been created by divine power." [1] By this act of faith, history is declared to be man's area of operation exclusive of any divine determination or operation.

Having made this assumption, these scholars then proceed to apply it to history. History becomes simply men's development and struggling in a mindless universe. This application is then taken as "proof" or the assumption which produced this view! Clearly, this is circular reasoning: it is reasoning from faith to faith, and it is guilty of the very process of which it accuses the Christian.

A classic example of this is Auguste Comte's (1798–1857) "Law of Three Stages" in *The Positive Philosophy.* Comte denied God; therefore God's presence in history was mythological, and progress in history was progress from theology

---

[1] This translation is given by Gordon H. Clark: *A Christian Philosophy of Education,* p. 31, Grand Rapids: Eerdmans, 1946. This sentence from *De Rerum Nature* I, 148-150, is given in John Selby Watson's *Lucretius on The Nature of Things* (Bohn's Classical Library, 1904), p. 10, as "our first principle shall hence take its commencement, THAT NOTHING IS EVER DIVINELY GENERATED FROM NOTHING."

to positivistic science. The three stages through which each branch of knowledge passes are therefore the Theological or fictitious; the Metaphysical or abstract; and the Scientific or positive. Man passes from a desire for meaning to a pragmatic recognition that meaning does not exist and reality must therefore be approached methodologically and pragmatically. By this simple scheme Comte applied the doctrine of social evolution (which long preceded biological evolution) to history and relegated theology to the age of myth. That Comte's general schema is still so extensively held is evidence of the power of faith over fact, because history quite clearly gives a very different picture.

We can, with a rough accuracy and for convenience, rather divide the development of thought into three very different stages as *thus far* apparent in history. The *first* stage of human thought was the *politico-magical* worldview. Apart from the Hebrews, this perspective governed all of antiquity, and it governed the Roman Empire in the Christian era and continued thereafter to govern the non-Christian world. In order to understand the significance of the politico-magical world view, it is important to know what magic is. This requires a distinction between the technique and the purpose of magic. All too commonly, magic is defined in terms of its primitive techniques and thereby exorcised from the modern world view. But magic is better defined in terms of its purpose; the techniques have varied from culture to culture, but the purpose remains unchanged. The purpose of magic is to gain autonomous control over man, nature, and the supernatural, control over the totality of whatever really exists and however it may be defined. Modern science, having steadily forsaken its Christian origins, is governed increasingly by magic, by a desire for a total control over reality. In the Biblical perspective, science is a necessary activity of the godly man and society as they seek to understand and subdue the earth

101

under God and in obedience to His creation mandate. In the magical faith, man aims at total control in contempt, defiance, and unbelief of God.

From the beginning of history, one of the best, if not the easiest, means of exercising this control has been through political control. As a result, magic and politics early made an alliance. And the consequence was that, *in antiquity, salvation was not religious; salvation was political.* Religion was a subordinate aspect of ancient life and simply a department of state, a division of public welfare and public works. Man's basic orientation was political; one can say that his religion was politics, if we use religion as the vehicle of salvation. The state and its rulers, in this politico-magical world view, were in some sense divine: they were the controllers of the totality of reality. The politico-magical world-view thus supplanted God and religion with a totalitarian magical order.

Even a cursory glance at ancient and non-Christian cultures reveals the prevalence of this politico-magical perspective. Baal worship in the Middle East was the worship of lords, natural and political, who governed all reality. The political rulers readily adopted Baalism in order to command that total control offered by this politico-magical world view. Moloch worship, with its demand for human sacrifice, was politico-magical, and Moloch literally meant "king." The medicine men of American Indian tribes had little relationship to religion; their function was magical, and medicine was one facet of their claimed control over reality. The attempts by caesaro-papism to absorb the Christian Church represent attempts to reduce the church to an aspect of the politico-magical order as against allowing the church freedom to smash that order and remake it into a religious one.

The *second* stage of human thought has been the religious or Christian one. With the coming of Christ, the religious stage, previously largely restricted to the Hebrews, now moved out to command the world. The result was the immediate warfare of Christ and the caesars, an all-out battle between the politico-magical world view and the Biblical world view. It is the custom now of the new mythologists to treat the Roman persecution of the Christians as largely legendary. The reality is very different. An attempt was made by Rome to wipe out Christianity. At first, it was through the judicial murder of selected members and leaders. Finally, it was the attempted mass murder of an entire people. It was a long and ugly battle, but the Empire, though possessing the power of the sword and using it very savagely, finally lost.

In Jesus Christ, life was restored from a politico-magical world view to a religious one. In Adam's fall, his attempt to be as God (Gen. 3:5), the politico-magical perspective was born. In Christ's temptation, the politico-magical world view was met and conquered. Life and salvation were restored to a religious dimension.

The result was a new historiography. The older historiography was singularly barren. It simply narrated the possession of *power* and was antiquarian in all things else. Instead of *movement* and *progress* in history, ancient history simply cited *power* and *control*. St. Augustine pointed to the conflict of history, between the City of God and the City of Man, between Biblical religion, between Christianity, and the politico-magical order. History therefore has a purpose, the triumph of the heavenly city, and history therefore is capable of progress. There is development in both cities, as each works out the implications of its presuppositions. The only development Plato could envision was one of greater controls over man, a communistic order, because his perspective was politico-magical. In Augustine, the goal is open to the imagination: the cities will grow, not in controls, but in their epistemological self-consciousness, and the future is therefore both certain and unknown. The

103

progress of Western history is unique in world history; it is simply a product of the triumph of the Biblical world view, the supplanting of the politico-magical orders with the Christian religion.

The *third* stage is now in evidence, the attempt to restore the politico-magical world view. The Christian world view has been introduced extensively in every continent. The slumbering politico-magical lions are everywhere aroused. In Western culture, they have been active, in the neo-platonist revivals, Aristotelianism, the Renaissance, and the Enlightenment. The United Nations today is a politico-magical world order, and virtually all nations are also. The churches have been largely captured by magic and accordingly have a social or political gospel. Salvation has once again become political, and Christian salvation is denounced savagely as irrelevant and obscurantist. The battle is joined between the state as god and God as God.

It is therefore not presumptuous to posit the rise of still another stage, since God is God and shall prevail: a triumphant Christian order across the earth, and the suppression of the politico-magical world view. Since God has everything to do with history, its every tomorrow is in terms of Him. There is no other history.

XI

THE VIRGIN BIRTH AND HISTORY

Few things are more staggering than the audacity of unbelief. The atheist hates God; therefore, there is no God; he finds miracles an offense; therefore, by definition miracles are an impossibility. And, in particular, as the atheist and the agnostic approach the Biblical narrative of the virgin birth, they talk with pseudo-learnedness of myth and legendary accretions. But the narrative, from start to finish, is not only carefully historical, but it affirms a philosophy of history which is the negation of myth.

The essence of the narrative is that the sovereign and ultimate being, God, became incarnate, was born of the Virgin Mary, in order to establish God's salvation and kingship in history and over history.

The Annunciation (Luke 1:26-38) declared that Jesus would be the Son of God, and the son of David, born very God of very God, and very man of very man. He is identified both as the eternal king, and as the promised messianic king. The purpose therefore of His coming is not mythical but historical: it is to accomplish in history the purposes of God. The myth seeks an escape from history: it is offered as a means of overcoming and ending history. The Annunciation declares rather the coming of Jesus as the one through whom history is to develop to its logical and necessary conclusion, the Kingdom of God. Hence the intensely historical perspective of both Matthew's and Luke's accounts of the virgin birth.

The problem for the critics is not in the narrative so much as in the God of the narrative, the sovereign God with whom "nothing shall be impossible" (Luke 1:37).

To continue with Luke's account, as the more detailed one, the Magnificat (Luke 1:46-58) is a triumphant affirmation of faith concerning history. Mary views the coming birth of her son as a triumph in history. She exalts the name of the Lord, because He is fulfilling His promises made unto the forefathers. Through the Messiah, God is preparing to dethrone all His enemies, avenge His suffering saints, and show the strength of His arm. A reading of the Magnificat is instructive:

> My soul doth magnify the Lord,
> And my spirit hath rejoiced in God my Saviour.
> For he hath regarded the low estate of his handmaiden: for behold, from henceforth all generations shall call me blessed.
> For he that is mighty hath done to me great things; and holy is his name.
> And his mercy is on them that fear him from generation to generation.
> He hath shewed strength with his arm; he hath scattered the proud in the imagination of their hearts.
> He hath put down the mighty from their seats, and exalted them of low degree.
> He hath filled the hungry with good things; and the rich he hath sent empty away.
> He hath holpen his servant Israel, in remembrance of his mercy;
> As he spake to our fathers, to Abraham, and to his seed for ever.

We have spoken of the audacity of unbelief. It is of two kinds. *First*, there are those who deny the virgin birth and all that it means. *Second*, there are those who affirm the virgin birth but not what it means.

To illustrate: Mary has described what the coming of

the Son does to history: it is nothing less than the total overturning and redirection of all things. The major step in this overturning is the coming of the Son; after that, all things else follow inevitably in the course of time, so that they can be spoken of as in effect already accomplished. Arndt admits that the Magnificat means that "through the Messiah, God will dethrone all enemies." [1] This is well stated; the Magnificat can mean little else. Then what shall we say, when Arndt adds later (with reference to 1:52), "In my opinion the meaning of the words of Mary is exclusively spiritual," and adds as proof, "The coming of Jesus did not abolish political tyrannies and earthly poverty."[2] Is this not likewise a form of unbelief, and a rejection of history? Does it not reduce Christ to the role of a mythical hero come to rescue man from history? What point then in the incarnation and in the bodily resurrection, if the world is to be written off as the realm of the devil, as historically irrecoverable?

Luther saw the Magnificat as describing six works of God in history: *first*, mercy; *second*, God breaks down spiritual pride; *third*, He puts down the mighty; *fourth*, He exalts the lowly; *fifth and sixth*, God fills the hungry with good things, and the rich He hath sent empty away. Commenting on the third, Luther said:

> For He does not destroy the mighty as suddenly as they deserve, but lets them go for a season, until their might has reached its highest point. When it has done this, God does not support it, neither can it support itself; it breaks down of its own weight without any crash or sound, and the oppressed are raised up, also without any sound, for God's strength is in them, and it alone remains when the strength of the mighty has fallen.

Observe, however, that Mary does not say He breaks the

[1] William F. Arndt: *The Gospel According to St. Luke*, p. 60. St. Louis, Missouri: Concordia, 1956.
[2] *Ibid.*, p. 62.

107

seats, but He casts the mighty from their seats. Nor does she say He leaves those of low degree in their low degree, but He exalts them. For while the world stands, authority, rule, power, and seats must remain.[3]

In his "Epilog" to the Magnificat, Luther addressed John Frederick (1503–1554), the Elector's nephew, with these plain words:

Your Grace should reflect that in all the Scriptures God did not permit any heathen king or prince throughout the length or breadth of the world to be praised, but, contrariwise, to be punished; this is a mighty and terrible example to all rulers. Moreover, even in Israel, His chosen people, He never found a king worthy of praise and not rather of punishment. . . .

All these things were foreordained by God in order to terrify those in authority, to keep them in fear, and to admonish them of their peril.[4]

Arndt called himself Lutheran, but Martin Luther obviously saw no exclusively spiritual meaning in the Magnificat.

Similarly, John Calvin saw the Magnificat in terms of history, and he compared the worldly powers of the Christian era to the tower of Babel builders, whom God through Mary declared He would forever confound:

He hath scattered the proud in the thought of their heart. This expression is worthy of notice: for as their pride and ambition are outrageous, as their covetousness is insatiable, they pile up their deliberations to form an immense heap, and, to say all in a single word, they build the tower of Babel (Gen. xi.9). Not satisfied with having made one or another foolish attempt beyond their strength, or with their former schemes of mad presumption, they still add to their amount. When God has for a time looked down from heaven, in silent mockery, on their splendid preparations, he unexpectedly scatters the whole mass: just as when a building is overturned, and

[3] Jaroslav Pelikan, editor: *Luther's Works*, vol. 21, p. 343f. St. Louis: Concordia, 1956.
[4] *Ibid.*, p. 356f.

its parts, which had formerly been bound together by a strong and firm union, are widely scattered in every direction.[5]

Throughout his commentary, Calvin very plainly saw the Magnificat as a revelation concerning history, a declaration that God governs history absolutely, and the incarnation is a declaration of His sovereign and redeeming power.

Thus, when Mary says, that it is God who *casteth down nobles from their thrones, and exalteth mean persons,* she teaches us, that the world does not move and revolve by a blind impulse of Fortune, but that all the revolutions observed in it are brought about by the Providence of God, and that those judgments, which appear to us to disturb and overthrow the entire framework of society, are regulated by God with unerring justice. This is confirmed by the following verse, *He hath filled the hungry with good things, and hath sent the rich away empty. . . .* To such godly persons as feel poverty and almost famine, and lift up their cry to God, no small consolation is afforded by this doctrine, that he *filleth the hungry with good things.*[6]

As surely as we beware of the atheists, so must we beware of the unbelief of snivelling preachers who reduce the relevance of the virgin birth to the spiritual realm, who deny its relevance to history, for the Magnificat declares that God has brought salvation to the whole world of man, material and spiritual, religious, political, and economic, and let those who deny this confess their unbelief. The joy of Mary is in the salvation of God, a mighty reversal of all things, of all human values, powers, and plans by God our Savior. The Old Testament promises to the faithful seed are being fulfilled.

In the Benedictus (Luke 1:67-80), this note of triumph in history is carried further. Zacharias rejoiced in the

[5] John Calvin: *Commentary on a Harmony of the Evangelists,* I, p. 58. Grand Rapids: Eerdmans, 1949.
[6] *Ibid.,* p. 60.

fact that God keeps His promises, "as he spake by the mouth of holy prophets" (Luke 1:70, 72, 73). A kinsman redeemer has come, God incarnate as man's next-of-kin and redeemer (vv. 68, 72). We are "saved from our enemies and from the hand of all that hate us" (v. 71); the meaning is obviously not "spiritual"! The religious salvation through this God-man is cited as being remission of sins, and the mercy or grace of God.

Jesus Christ is called the "dayspring" in the Benedictus, i.e., the rising sun or Sun of righteousness (Mal. 4:2), who gives "light to them that sit in darkness and in the shadow of death, to guide our feet into the way of peace" (Luke 1:78f). The figure is a striking one. Prior to Jesus Christ, the movement of history was meager, and in the dark. The pilgrims of history were afraid to move; they could not move, having no direction in the dark. The movement of history was God's movement, the Biblical revelation. Now, with the fulness of the revelation, God's people move with Him in the light of Christ. According to the Benedictus, the great forward movement of man in history began in Christ and with Christ.

Much more can be said. Suffice it to say that every aspect of the nativity narrative is not only historical but directed towards the fulfilment of the historical process. Unbelievers will revert to the pagan cyclical view of history, which is in effect a denial of relevance to history. And Christians who fail to see the historical relevance of the nativity will have little relevance to history. The modern "spiritualizing" of the prophecies of the nativity is a witness to the impotence of the contemporary church. As has been noted, there is no such perversion of Scripture and surrender of history in Luther and in Calvin.

110

XII

THE DENIAL OF HISTORY BY THE HISTORIANS

To accept myth is to reject history, and to make myths the premise in terms of which history is judged is to deny any validity to history.

The presuppositions of historians are therefore of the utmost importance. Is the historian governed by myth, and, if so, by what myth? His learning may be massive, his scholarship ponderous, but the net result may be futile if his governing principle is myth. Isaiah's comment on certain leaders of his age is appropriate: "You are pregnant with chaff, you shall bring forth stubble" (Isa. 33:11, Smith-Goodspeed version). Those who live in terms of myth are like the ones who writhed in labor but "gave birth only to wind" (Isa. 26:18, Smith-Goodspeed).

To avoid myth, a historian must disavow the cult of "objective, impartial" scholarship. The historian is not God. He is not beyond history; he is not transcendental. The historian views history from a time, place, and philosophical perspective, and his report is conditioned by these things. To deny to the historian the possibility of infallibility is not to ascribe to him the certainty of falsification, i.e., a kind of inverse infallibility which dooms him to the certainty of error. The historian's report represents a perspective on history, and it is a limited perspective of necessity, but it can still be, within these limits, a notably true and faithful report.

But there is a diminishing possibility of any true history

to the measure that the historian is governed by myth. And myth, unhappily, governs most historians today.

Let us examine a particular but commonplace example, from a widely honored, published and republished book by a major historian, Kenneth M. Stampp's *The Peculiar Institution, Slavery in the Ante-Bellum South.* In the preface, Stampp makes a remarkable statement, and the paragraph deserves full citation:

> Yet there is a strange paradox in the historian's involvement with both present and past, for his knowledge of the present is clearly a key to his understanding of the past. Today we are learning much from the natural and social sciences about the Negro's potentialities and about the basic irrelevance of race, and we are slowly discovering the roots and meaning of human behavior. All this is of immense value to the historian when, for example, he tries to grasp the significance of the Old South's "peculiar institution." I have assumed that the slaves were merely human beings, that innately Negroes are, after all, only white men with black skins, nothing more, nothing less. This gives quite a new and different meaning to the bondage of black men; it gives their story a relevance to men of all races which it never seemed to have before.[1]

By this statement, Stampp has asserted his humanism; he has also let us know that he believes himself to have a heart full of love and respect for all men. But has he not also denied that he is an historian?

If Negroes are only "white men with black skins, nothing more, nothing less," then conversely white men are only Negroes with white skins, nothing more, nothing less. This means that all cultural differences, hereditary predispositions, and historical traditions are irrelevant and meaningless. It means, in other words, that *history* is meaningless.

[1] Kenneth M. Stampp: *The Peculiar Institution, Slavery in the Ante-Bellum South,* pp. vii-viii. New York: Vintage Books, A Division of Random House, 1956; originally published by A. A. Knopf.

And how can one be an historian if it is his purpose to deny history?

The white man has behind him centuries of Christian culture, and the discipline and selective breeding this faith requires. Although the white man may reject this faith and subject himself instead to the requirements of humanism, he is still a product of this Christian past. The Negro is a product of a radically different past, and his heredity has been governed by radically different considerations. Elizabeth E. Hoyt has cited Dr. Simon Biesheuvel's comparisons, a deliberately extreme contrast to pinpoint certain cultural ideas, African and Western. From Tennyson's *Ulysses* is cited "a typically Western expression of man's purpose":

> To follow knowledge like a sinking star,
> Beyond the utmost bounds of human thought . . .
>
> To sail beyond the sunset, and the baths
> Of all the Western stars, until I die . . .
>
> To strive, to seek, to find, and not to yield.

By contrast, illustrating what Africans call Negritude, is "the following cry from Aimee Cesaire of Martinique":

> Hurray for those who have never invented anything.
> Hurray for those who have never explored anything.
> Hurray for those who have never conquered anything.
> But who in awe give themselves up to the essence of things.
> Ignorant of the shell, but seized by the rhythm of things.
> Not intent on conquest, but playing the play of the world.[2]

This contrast is an over-simplification, and one designed

[2] Elizabeth E. Hoyt, "The Family of Mankind: Some New Light?" in *Mankind Quarterly*, vol. II, no. 1, July-September, 1961, p. 14. Hoyt is a member of the Economics Department of Iowa State University.

to be flattering to both races, but it does indicate the reality of racial differences. Men like Stampp would, of course, seek to negate every historical citation of differences as merely "cultural differences." The men behind the respective cultures are the same men. It is therefore held to be wrong to cite histories against any race.

A more absurd position can scarcely be imagined. If you and I have our histories abstracted from us, and our heredities as well, and all our cultural conditioning and responses, we are no longer men, no longer human beings, but an abstract and theoretical concept of man. No real history of us can then be written. Stampp's Negroes are thus neither black men nor white men; they are an abstraction; Stampp's white slave-owners are also an abstraction, but an abstraction to illustrate the devil in Stampp's humanistic morality play. The result is not history: it is a modern *Everyman,* a morality play that parades as history. But, more than that, it is a denial of history because it regards the abstractions as real, and reality as trivial and unreal. The humanistic historian thus has revived universalism on new terms: his abstractions are the realities, the universals, the true order of reality, whereas the everyday world of history represents simply the sorry accidental world of particulars and of unreality. The basic premise of such thinking is Hellenic, and Hellenism could not produce a valid historiography because it denied the validity of history. Christianity made historiography possible, and the return to abstract universals can only destroy history, even as the medieval adoption of Aristotle destroyed both that era and its sense of history.

Regrettably Stampp is not alone. Virtually every historian today approaches history with the sorry universals of a post-Hegelian, post-Marxian era. In their political hopes, and in their historiography, they seek to end history.

The results of this new universalism are often amusing

in the radical blindness to history it engenders. We are told that, in an area of New Guinea "only recently weaned from head-hunting" and still very primitive, a visiting United Nations delegate travelled through the district and "is said to have enquired critically why no university had yet been put up for the Kanakas." [3] Such men cannot see headhunters: they see only their abstraction, their universal man. And men who are blind to history cannot write it, but they do become victims to it.

[3] From a book review of Rene Gardi: *Tombaran: An Encounter With Cultures in Decline in New Guinea*, in *Mankind Quarterly*, vol. V, no. 2, October-December, 1964, p. 119.

XIII

THE TREE OF LIFE

A basic concept in the political philosophy of the ancient world was the tree of life. The Assyrian monarchs, for example, were depicted as officiating before a garlanded pole or ritual "tree" which represented the ritual center of the earth.[1] The pole or tree was the tree of life, "a symbol of the life-giving functions of the king."[2] Another "symbol of divine kingship" was the bull[3] (or golden calf). The king represented the manifest divinity of the cosmos and its present power and dominion. The central manifestation of divinity was thus in the state, in particular in the dominant empire, so that this divine order as it appeared in the state and the monarch was the tree of life to its age. May Day in Rome and elsewhere represented this same faith, and Roman women on the first of May made offerings to Bona Dea, the good goddess, or "the earth," and the name May perhaps came from Majores or Maiores, the older branch of the Senate, i.e., the source of power.[4] The Maypole was a representation of the tree of life. The center of the earth, thus, was the empire, and it was the divinity of

[1] Eric Burrows, "Some Cosmological Patterns in Babylonian Religion," in S. H. Hooke, editor: *The Labyrinth, Further Studies in the Relation between Myth and Ritual in the Ancient World*, p. 63n. London: SPCK, 1935.

[2] S. H. Hooke: *The Siege Perilous, Essays in Biblical Anthropology*, p. 137; cf. 125. London: SCM Press, 1956.

[3] *Ibid.*, p. 25.

[4] Maymie R. Krythe: *All About the Months*, p. 88. New York: Harper and Row, 1966.

the age, its tree of life and source of fertility. The pagan roots of socialism and humanistic law are apparent in their deliberate use of May Day to celebrate their new order. Called Law Day by bar associations, May Day represents the establishment of humanistic and anti-Christian law.

The tree of life was thus a familiar image to the ancient world. Nebuchadnezzar's dream of his future portrayed him as a tree of life hewn down (Dan. 4). The Bible first refers to the tree of life in Genesis 2:9, and again in Genesis 3: 22, 24. The reference is to a literal tree, but a tree having a sacramental significance and denoting the gift of eternal life in consequence of faith and obedience. When man submitted to the desire to be his own god, his own principle of ultimacy, and his arbiter of good and evil, he was cut off from that life-giving communion. The consequence of his sin was spiritual separation from God, and the outcome of separation, the inevitable liability to death. In Proverbs 3:18, "Wisdom," a person of the Godhead, is called "a tree of life to them that lay hold" of Wisdom. In Ezekiel 47:12, there is a reference to the tree of life as the principle of health and salvation for the messianic age. Jesus Christ, in Revelation 2:7, promises the tree of life, "which is in the midst of the paradise of God, . . . to him that overcometh." In Revelations 22:2, the tree of life is a product of God and Christ, nourished by the "pure river of waters of life" (22:1), and its purpose is "the healing of the nations" or peoples (22:2). "Blessed are they that do his commandments, that they may have right to the tree of life, and may enter in through the gates into the city" (22:14), i.e., into the New Jerusalem, the City of God, the true order.

Without entering into further theological identification of the tree of life, it can be said that it is, *first*, closely linked or identified with God. *Second*, as closely identified with divinity, it is thus the source of life, order, communion or society, and law. *Third*, it is at the heart of God's community,

117

the Garden or Paradise, seen in its fulness as both the Garden and the City, so that without the tree there is no Kingdom, only death.

The Biblical faith was basically accepted by pagan antiquity but simply transposed. Heaven and earth were united into one cosmos in origin. According to a fragment of Euripides' *The Wise Melanippe*, "heaven and earth were one form; then they were separated from one another, they engendered and bore all things and brought to light plants, birds, animals and the creatures nourished by the sea water, and the race of mortals." [5] The purpose of the state was to re-establish the necessary unity and order by making itself the bond of heaven and earth, the tree of life to its people. The state thus became the life-giving tree to its age and citizenry. However, since creation was formed by the separation and consequent hostility and interaction of heaven and earth, social order rested not only on the supremacy of the state as the principle of unity and order, but on the ritual invocation of periodic chaos as the source of fertility. Thus, *first*, the state represented the bond of heaven and earth, the unification of the cosmos into its true order, and the state was thus the tree of life to its people. However, *second*, since the fertility of creation was a product of chaos, the state could not deny chaos. Out of the rending of the original order, the world of living things had been born; therefore chaos represented fertility, vigor, creativity. Accordingly, the state as the tree of life invoked chaos in periodic festivals, such as Saturnalia, in revolutionary activity aimed at overthrowing periodically the threat of sterility through order, or as a result of order.

There was thus a legitimacy of chaos, and this legitimacy was in two spheres. First, chaos was legitimate and neces-

[5] Hans Leisegang, "The Mystery of the Serpent," in Joseph Campbell, editor: *Pagan and Christian Mysteries, Papers from the Eranos Yearbooks*, p. 12. New York: Harper Torchbooks, 1963 (1955).

sary at the time of the festival, when acts of incest, homo-sexuality, and coition with animals was often required to revitalize the state. Second, this legitimate chaos could occur outside the state, in relationship to non-members of the state, so that, as social revitalization took place in the festival, personal revitalization was possible with slaves and foreigners, persons legally outside the state and in the world of chaos, i.e., not under the protecting sovereignty of the messianic state. This appears very clearly, for example, in the following Hittite laws:

194: If a free man cohabits with (several) slave-girls, sisters and their mother, there shall be no punishment. If blood-relations sleep with (the same) free woman, there shall be no punishment. If father and son sleep with (the same) slave-girl or harlot, there shall be no punishment.

195: If however a man sleeps with the wife of his brother while his brother is living, it is a capital crime. If a man has a free woman (in marriage) and then lies also with her daughter, it is a capital crime. If a man has the daughter in marriage and then lies also with her mother or her sister, it is a capital crime.

200 (A): If a man does evil with a horse or a mule, there shall be no punishment. He must not appeal to the king nor shall he become a case for the priest.—If any-one sleeps with a foreign (woman) and (also) with her mother or (her) si(ster), there will be no punishment.[6]

The only unusual feature of this Hittite law is that it both-ered to specify that such relations were outside the law and legitimate acts of chaos. In virtually all cultures, the slave and foreigner had no relationships to the state, the tree of life, and hence were legitimate objects of acts of social, sexual, and material chaos. Biblical law placed all men equally under God's law, because Biblical law derives from

[6] James Prichard, editor: *Ancient Near Eastern Texts*, p. 196f. Second edition. Princeton: Princeton University Press, 1955.

the sovereign God, not from a state and its citizenry; Biblical law protects God's order, not the social order of a people and their state. Whenever and wherever law in its point of ultimate and essential origin moves from God to man, the state becomes man's tree of life, in that collective man in the form of the state is now his own principle of order. And to be the principle of order means also to be the principle of power, because order has behind it *the power* to maintain an order, and *the authority* to do so by right. Power is now identified with authority, and both are seen as humanistic concepts.

As a result, as Bertrand Russell suggested in *Power*, the basic unifying force for society and for the social sciences is power, and the phenomenon of social power is the basic subject of concern for social scientists. As a Negro scholar, Dr. Kenneth B. Clark, has noted, power appears in its use without talk of power; those who speak of it, as Stokely Carmichael on "Black Power," give "a pathetic demonstration of the lack of any effective power. Verbal, emotional slogans may be seen as forms of pseudo-power which attempt to substitute for and operate as if they were real." [7] Clark's definition of social power is simply that power is power:

> The model for a social science definition of "social power" comes directly from physics, the definition of power as found in the sphere of physical energy and matter. And the simplest definition which I could find is the one I latched onto for my purposes, namely, power defined as any form of energy or force required or available for work to bring about motion or pressure. I think that definition can be used quite directly in social science. By social power, then, we mean that energy or force or a combina-

[7] Kenneth B. Clark: *Social Power and Social Change in Contemporary America*, p. 7. U. S. Dept. of State Publication 8125, September, 1966, Office of Equal Opportunity. Clark sees the present day as one when for the intellectual Negro a happy situation prevails: it is "popular to be a Negro and sought after," p. 8.

tion of forces required to bring about, to sustain, or to prevent social, political, or economic change. This simplistic definition is based upon a number of assumptions: that social change or events or occurrences in a society, institutional changes, changes in the relationship among people, are controllable. These relationships may be facilitated or inhibited by human beings particularly by those human beings who have been given or who arrogate to themselves, and operate with impunity in terms of, the right, the privilege, or the status to make relevant decisions affecting the lives of other individuals. Obviously, those individuals with the unchallenged status to make such decisions, to implement such decisions, and to control the society in terms of their decisions and desires, are individuals with high status, and with power. High status and social power tend to go together.[8]

This is clearly a theological definition, even as definitions in physics have become theological. When any object is defined in terms of itself or by itself, without reference to anything else or to any norm, then that object has been made ultimate: it has become a god, beyond definition and itself a source of definition. For Clark, power is power, because power is ultimate; it is the god of his system. Where power is, there is the ritual center of his earth, and the tree of life in his system.

This, of course, means total relativism. It means, as Clark recognizes, that he cannot condemn "Hitler and Nazi Germany," or, we may add, white colonials or white slave-owners. He therefore qualifies power with a humanistic admonition: "That society is most stable and secure in which the leaders use no greater degree of power or force to maintain or modify the status quo than that which is required to obtain the desired results." [9] But by what standard does Clark do this? What principle of ultimacy has Clark established as a judge and god over power? Clark appeals to clinical psychology to

[8] *Ibid.*, p. 12.
[9] *Ibid.*, p. 13.

call pathological the expending of "greater energy in behavior or interpersonal relations than that which is ordinarily required." [10] But again what is Clark's standard of normal and abnormal power?

Social power, Clark holds, "can be used either to maintain a status quo, or to modify it, or to change it fundamentally." The use of social power to maintain an order is conservatism, and Clark lists as conservative groups the NAACP, the Urban League, "and to some extent a pre-McKissick CORE . . . , because they are not requiring, they are not demanding that the social system, the power system, be changed fundamentally. They were not even requiring that it be modified too significantly, except from the point of view of the resistant extreme white." [11]

Clark further holds that equality is basic to power, because it "is my belief that there is something about social power that apparently makes it not adaptive if there is too great a disequilibrium within a given social system." [12]

What Clark has essentially said is, *first*, that since for him there is no God, all men are gods and all men should have power. This means equality. *Second*, the state should thus use power to achieve a society of equality, and the use of power to this end is legitimate power. *Third*, use of power to frustrate this would thus be illegitimate. But Clark does not elevate equality as a god over power; for him equality remains as an aspect of power in its truest democratic sense, in that power is an expression implicitly of the general will of the people. Power remains basic, but power now appears as a two-faced god, a kind of Janus, both god and devil in its various aspects, both the tree of life and the tree of death.

Since there is no transcendence in this system, no god

10 *Ibid.*
11 *Ibid.*, p. 14.
12 *Ibid.*, p. 18.

beyond man and the state, ethics gives way to aesthetics as the basis of life. When man is his own god, he is beyond good and evil. The decisions of life are then no longer questions of morality but matters of taste. Accordingly, as Read has pointed out, "art should be the basis of education." [13] Man's nature is one of "natural neutrality." [14] The concepts of good and bad are arbitrary and disruptive; they are "induced into the mind of the child" by false education. "The result is a state of psychic ambivalence peculiarly liable to tensions (psychoses) and disruptions (neuroses) in the individual, and a state of unconsciousness in society equally fraught with the possibilities of breakdown (revolts and wars)." [15] In effect, the restoration of man to the tree of life involves therefore the abolition of God, and of the concepts of good and evil. The goal is "the city of man." [16] Even Pope Paul VI has made "the cult of man" one of the "Christian principles." [17]

As a result of all these things, life again, as in the ancient world, has become politicized. Everything now is a part of the sphere of politics and under the jurisdiction of the state, because politics is salvation, and outside the sovereign state there is no salvation for man. If there are storms and bad weather, an appropriation by the state for weather control is the answer. The modern prayer to god concerning weather is a petition to the sovereign state. In the United States, in 1967, federal planning weather-modification grants were to reach nearly $150 million a year by 1970, with the goals being enhanced rainfall, and "ways to dissipate fog, sup-

[13] Herbert Read: *Education Through Art*, p. 1. New York: Pantheon, Third edition, 1956.

[14] *Ibid.*, p. 4.

[15] *Ibid.*, p. 276.

[16] Barbara Ward: *Spaceship Earth*, p. 16. New York: Columbia University Press, 1966.

[17] John G. Clancy, editor: *Dialogues. Reflections on God and Man by Paul VI*, p. 181. The Credo Series. New York: Pocket Books, 1965.

press hail, stop lightning, stifle tornadoes and de-energize hurricanes." [18] Poverty, disease, earthquakes, crime, wars, every problem of man is referred to the sovereign state for solution, because political man sees the sovereign state as his savior and the tree of life.

When the pagan state of the ancient world declared itself to be the tree of life, it affirmed thereby its belief that it had seized the power and the glory of God and now commanded history. History was therefore to be understood, not in terms of God but in terms of man, not from the perspective of eternity but from the perspective of time. These ancient monarchs, states, and empires are gone; their "command" of history proved illusory, and their interpretation false. Their modern successors, with their similar dreams, and their hope of a one-world state as man's hope and "tree of life," are doomed to the same defeat, and they give every evidence of a much shorter life-span of truth and pretention than their ancient predecessors. As the Psalmist declared, "The LORD reigneth; let the people tremble: he sitteth between the cherubims; let the earth be moved" (Ps. 99:1; in the Berkeley Version, "The LORD is King; let the nations tremble!"). For God, the outcome of history is a foregone conclusion. "There are many devices in a man's heart; nevertheless, the counsel of the LORD, that shall stand" (Prov. 19:21).

[18] "Something Is Wrong with the Weather," *U. S. News & World Report*, July 10, 1967, vol. LXIII, no. 2, p. 40.

APPENDIX 1

AMERICAN HISTORY: MEANING AND RESOURCES

Recently, an officer of the American Historical Association called attention to the irrelevance of so much of the work of professional historians:

> We seem at times to care little about the meanings and values of our discipline, to devote ourselves too exclusively to the piling up of information on more and more minute and perhaps less and less significant subjects. There is nothing wrong certainly with research or with accumulation of facts. But the piling up of information on more and more specialized subjects is only worthwhile if the heaping leads to more than just more. . . . It is time, I think, that we ask ourselves again and forcefully if learning is simply the accumulation of information or if it also calls for judgment, evaluation, and determination of meaning for other individuals and for our society. Can we any longer believe with the positivists that all we have to do is to discover facts, that the facts will, in some mysterious way, speak for themselves, that when we have enough facts we will somehow arrive at philosophical truth, and a golden age? The greater historians have not so believed, nor really, do many of us now so believe.[1]

A concern with meaning, values and history is not new. Biblical faith has made a Christian-theistic ethical concern central to Western culture. In recent years, scientific philosophical and sociological approaches have not been lacking. In 1902, Heinrich Rickert wrote what has recently been trans-

---

[1] Boyd C. Shafer, "History, Not Art, Not Science, But History: Meanings and Uses of History," in *Pacific Historical Review*, vol. XXIX, no. 2, May, 1960, p. 168f.

lated as *Science and History, A Critique of Positivist Episte-
mology.* Two works edited by Helmut Schoeck and James W.
Wiggins, *Scientism and Values* (1960) and *Relativism and the
Study of Man* (1961), give very able consideration to the
same problem. Bert James Lowenberg, in "Some Problems
Raised by Historical Relativism," [2] showed like concern over
the problem. But the problem grows more acute. Too many
historians are either given to a pessimistic, pagan cyclical
view of history as an endless repetition without direction or
meaning, or to relativism.[3] If life has no meaning, how can
history have any meaning? Does it not then merely become
a power play and "a tale told by an idiot, signifying
nothing"?

Attempts have been made to find refuge at least in "the
facts" of history. But, as one scholar has pointed out, there
are no self-contained facts: every fact points beyond itself
and is not capable of comprehension in terms of itself only.
The alternative then has been sought in experience: but
again experience points beyond itself. Our experience is
meaningless as sheer experience: meaning transcends our
experience. "Either way we attempt to discover the non-
systemic, non-cognitive, primitive factual or experiential
basis of knowledge, there is an inescapable and ultimate
relativity." [4] Facts, says Proctor, are no answer, and neither
is experience: both point beyond themselves. There is no
attempt to give the obvious answer, given by Christian
faith, and formulated in the philosophies of Cornelius Van
Til and Herman Dooyeweerd, that meaning always escapes
man when he seeks it in the realm of creation rather than
God. Because all things are made by God, nothing is under-

[2] *The Journal of Modern History*, vol. XXI, no. 1, March, 1949,
pp. 17-23.
[3] See Georg G. Iggers, "The Idea of Progress in Recent Philosophies of History," in *The Journal of Modern History*, vol. XXX, no. 3,
September, 1958, pp. 215-226.
[4] George L. Proctor, "The Concept of Fact in Recent Empiricism,"
in *Darshana*, vol. II, no. 3, August, 1962, p. 36.

standable in terms of itself but only in terms of God the Creator. No fact, nor man, can be understood in reference to itself alone, or to any created combination, but only in terms of God. Remove God, and, eventually, you remove meaning. John C. Greene has pointed out[5] that the idea of evolution is philosophical and means *progress*, which is a value-judgment. Attempts to "arrive at an objective, value-free definition of progress" soon fall. We can add that every attempt to do without God leads also to an elimination not only of values but of meaning as well. The issue is clear: no God, no meaning.

It becomes apparent then why many historians are unable to give coherence to their data: they have no concept of value, and hence no concept of meaning. If all things are relative, then they are also equally meaningless. Some historians, like Jacob Burckhardt, seek meaning in the past. Roots in the past are necessary, because without a consciousness of history, Burckhardt held, man is a barbarian.[6] And how does one give meaning to the past, lacking it in the present? History has been appealed to as a source of meaning, but, at the same time, relativism has depreciated the value of history and often reduced its standing as an academic discipline to an aspect of social studies. Meaning in history, and law in man's past, have been sometimes seen as fetters on his liberty, and rootlessness has been equated with freedom. But, modern psychiatry tells us, barbarians arise when life loses meaning and are bred in our very midst. How can the past be important if the present has no meaning? According to Christianity, man needs roots not only in the past but in the future; hope in Christ is "as an anchor of the soul" (Heb. 6:19), we are in Christ "begotten again unto a lively hope by the resurrec-

[5] "Evolution and Progress," in *Johns Hopkins Magazine*, vol. XIV, no. 1, October, 1962, pp. 8ff.
[6] Jacob Burckhardt: *Judgments on History and Historians*, p. 2. Boston: Beacon, 1958.

tion of Jesus Christ from the dead" (I Pet. 1:3), and are not as them "having no hope, and without God in the world" (Eph. 2:12). But positivists, after Comte, have steadily denied the relevance and importance of *meaning* in favor of *methodology*. It is thus assumed that educational methodology will in itself tend to educate, and that the form of democracy or of constitutionalism will create such orders in African states. *Methodology* has the dignity of science, whereas *meaning* suggests theology.

Having lost faith in a personal God, man's view of reality today is basically impersonal. As a consequence, he sees history, not in terms of a personal God, and personal man and his faith, but in terms of impersonal forces and drives. Both history and psychology are de-personalized and dehumanized. Since impersonal forces govern both man and history, the impetus for and faith in personal dedication and effort are nullified, and mass man is fostered. But James C. Malin, in *The Contriving Brain and the Skillful Hand* (1955), has stated that the "independence" of the United States in the 19th century was in part due to its theological cast of mind, which separated it from Enlightenment ideas. We can indeed affirm with Peter F. Drucker that the American Revolution was a conservative counter-revolution against such ideas. But to affirm this is to give new direction to American history studies, one in contradiction to most current work. There is on the whole an *avoidance* of this aspect of American history, and, in many major libraries, *limited resources* for its study.

A few illustrations can be given of this fact. Rev. John Witherspoon, president of Princeton (the College of New Jersey), a signer of the Declaration of Independence, and member of the Continental Congress, was a philosopher, theologian and economist whose influence on his pupils has been called very "profound" by Richard M. Gummere. His devoted students were influential in every area of life, and many were present in the Constitutional Convention. In subsequent United States history, one was president, another vice-president, ten were cabinet officers, twelve were governors, twenty-one senators, and thirty-nine congressmen. His influence on ministerial students was even more extensive. Here, clearly, was a man whose teaching guided a generation or more, and whose published works maintained that influence for some time. Now examine the materials available on Witherspoon at one of the major university libraries of the United States:

J. Witherspoon: *Lectures on Moral Philosophy.* This is not actually one of Witherspoon's books but the publication of a student's notes of a lecture series.

J. Witherspoon: *A Serious Inquiry into the Nature and Effect of the Stage.* A minor work, a long tract.

J. Witherspoon: "Public Credit Under the Confederation," a speech to the Continental Congress, calling for hard money, on the evils of paper and inflation, included in *World's Best Orations*, vol. X.

Butterfield: *John Witherspoon Comes to America, a Documentary Account*, 1953, 93 pp. Letters of Witherspoon at the time of his journey from Scotland to America.

Dodds, H. W.: "John Witherspoon, A Newcomen Address," Princeton University in the *Memorial Book of the Sesquicentennial of the Founding of the College of New Jersey.*

There are thus five items, no collected works, nothing of any real significance, the total amount adding up to one good book in bulk. There is thus *no attention* given to a major figure in American history whose influence on political theory and monetary policy, to cite but two areas, was very important. Again, the *resources* are lacking. Thus, there is neither the desire among scholars to work in this area, nor the resources collected for this purpose.

To cite another example, John Adams cited Hubert Languet's *Vindiciae Contra Tyrannos* as one of the most widely read and influential books in the colonies prior to the Revolution. A reading of *Vindiciae* and a study then of the concept of the *legality* of the Revolution as argued by the colnists and by their jurists makes clear the fact of agreement at the very least. This admitted classic is to be found in major libraries, but it is unused, and stands alone: there are no studies of it, or of its influence. Thomas Paine's works, of lesser importance (Paine landed in America *after* the Continental Congress had already been in session a few months) are mentioned in every high school history as a *cause* for what they followed after! And studies in Paine are many. But Paine was a Deist, Languet a Calvinist, and hence the neglect of *Vindiciae.* More than most of us realize, the current belief in historical studies of the "irrelevance" of Christian faith has been written into interpretations of American history. Where religion is seriously considered, it is too often seen as secondary to political, economic, and sociological factors, all real enough, but often seriously over-weighed.

American history studies are many, and Robert H. Walker, *American Studies in the United States* (1958), gives evidence of the extensive research being conducted. And yet much of this work is conducted in terms of relativistic, "scientific" or "liberal" ideas which are alien to any genuine appreciation of American history. Thus, when a scholar, writing in a major historical journal, cites "the national fetish of Constitution-worship" as a hindrance to historiography, and condemns an outstanding historian for being given to meaningless "abstractions" in speaking of violations of the constitution,[7] we know that the desired research is an exercise in historicism, that is, historical relativism. The terminology is revealing also: to call the regard for consti-

[7] Bernard A. Weisberger, "The Dark and Bloody Ground of Reconstruction Historiography," p. 442, in *The Journal of Southern History*, vol. XXV, no. 4, November, 1959.

tutionalism "worship" is scarcely an intelligent use of language, but to speak of this as a "national fetish" and equate the constitution thereby with a savage's cluster of feathers and charms is scarcely itself more than barbarism posing as scholarship. Thus, a disproportionate amount of recent American history has been debunking of one sort or another, or an attempt to answer such works. This is not to be confused with revisionism, a legitimate exercise. But it is significant even here that World War II revisionism, which would delineate the cynicism of recent political action, is extensively denied a hearing, whereas Radical Reconstruction revisionism, which would make meritorious the post-Civil War puppet regimes in the South, is very popular. Obviously, a political predisposition governs such attitudes, and cowardice in the face of present opposition.

As an instance of contemporary historical research at its very best, Forrest McDonald's *We the People, The Economic Origins of the Constitution* can be cited. Like Robert E. Brown's *Charles Beard and the Constitution*, it is concerned with analyzing Beard's theory of economic determinism. McDonald's research is nothing short of *extraordinary*. To answer the question, did the delegates approve the constitution in terms of their financial interests, he examines the background, properties, securities, and other interests of the constitutional convention. Members of every state ratification convention are also studied: what was their profession, landed property, livestock, slaves, kinds and amounts of securities, business properties, etc.? Except for a single work, all his sources were the original documents. He clearly disproves Beard's generalizations. But the question remains: was it worthwhile? We can be glad that all this information was made available for scholars, but what economic determinist has been convinced? And did not the rest of us already hold that man *cannot* live by bread or economic determinism alone? We are *not* told by what word, man's or God's, these founding fathers lived, and that is the important issue.

But some works deal with this, as witness Wilson Ober Clough's collection, *Intellectual Origins of American National Thought, Pages from the Books Our Founding Fathers Read* (1955). What *word* concerned these men? We find not a single colonial writer listed in the anthology! The Bible is cited once only, I Samuel 8. Greek, Roman, English, and Continental writers are cited as "origins" and the impression clearly given that the Revolution was born of the Enlightenment. But Louis I. Bredvold in *The Brave New World of the Enlightenment* (1961) has made clear that the Enlightenment is the source of modern totalitarianism, not liberty. Alice M. Baldwin, among others, made clear in 1928, in *The New England Clergy and the American Revolution*, the Christian source of the American Revolution and constitution. It is Clough's work, however, and not Baldwin's major search, which is used as a textbook. The reason is apparent in Carr, who himself shares these views of man's autonomy in history:

> The rationalists of the Enlightenment, who were the founders of modern historiography, retained the Jewish-Christian teleological view, but secularized the goal; they were thus enabled to restore the rational character of the historical process itself. History became progress towards the goal of the perfection of man's estate on earth.[8]

This "progress," as Bredvold has pointed out, was in terms of rational and scientific planning by an intellectual elite. *Modern historiography, being founded on the Enlightenment, moves in terms of a secular, Utopian and statist faith.* And some faith is necessary, as Carr himself states it:

> History properly so-called can be written only by those who find and accept a sense of direction in history itself.

[8] Edward Hallett Carr: *What Is History?*, p. 146. New York: Knopf, 1962.

The belief that we have come from somewhere is closely linked with the belief that we are going somewhere. A society which has lost belief in its capacity to progress in the future will quickly cease to concern itself with its progress in the past."

The dominant faith in historiography is Enlightenment faith, most clearly exemplified in Marxism: man plays god and remakes history in terms of total planning and control. The only effective challenge to this is the Christian one, and *the need is to develop a Christian historiography.* Rationalisic, anarchistic and "scientific" historiographies are only half-way houses to the Marxist enthronement of man the god-like planner.

Again American historians have neglected significant areas of history, even with respect to recent years. The number of works on the depression of the 1930's is very limited, but works published in America on Hitler are legion. And yet a case could be made for the fact that the serious, little-understood, and long-continued problems of the American economy contributed to the rise to power of Hitler. The Federal Reserve System has been described but inadequately analyzed, and this is true of many other major aspects of American economic history and monetary policy.

Moreover, many major and extensive influences have been neglected, and resource materials uncollected, because they involve either too "religious" a study, or branch off into political and economic theory as well as history. The influence of Fourier on such men as Considerant, Brisbane, and Horace Greeley needs extensive study. The influence of Swedenborg on such men as Emerson, Joseph Smith and Mormonism, and on American Socialism, goes completely unstudied, and yet Charles A. Dana, Assistant Secretary of War to Lincoln, editor of the New York *Tribune*, 1848–1862, and of the New York *Sun*, which he purchased in

" *Ibid.*, p. 176.

133

1867, could write of Swedenborg that he taught men "the laws of Divine Social order, and the re-integration of the Collective Man." In such editorials in one of America's major papers, Dana could propagate ideas that still remain unstudied despite their major influence.

Recently, important republication projects have been undertaken by various universities: Jonathan Edwards, Hamilton, Jefferson, Adams, and others. But much important work remains to be done yet. Moreover, too often there is a concentration on one man to the exclusion of others; their inter-relationships and influences on others are important. Thus, Edwards is important, but Joseph Bellamy and Samuel Hopkins had an extensive and continuing influence which is now forgotten. Their works are often missing from major libraries, and no attempt has been made to analyze, for example, Hopkins' influence, although Hildreth in 1849 credited Hopkins on the one hand and Unitarianism on the other with altering the New England character. Only recently has Gallatin's work as Secretary of the Treasury, 1801–1808, received attention, but from the critical perspective of Keynesian economics.[1] Gallatin's life has received more attention from scholars than the fiscal theories which made him important to U. S. history. Balinky, significantly, is not a historian but instead is an economist at Rutgers. Thus, historians, because of over-specialization, have by-passed in their studies of Gallatin the very thing which made him important because they had no competency in economics. This again points to a weakness in historiography. Certainly knowledge of theology, philosophy, political science, and economics is necessary to any understanding of history, but the average historian is intensive and circumscribed in his knowledge and hence unable to give perspective to his analysis. A fragmentation of history results.

[1] Alexander Balinky: *Albert Gallatin: Fiscal Theories and Policies.* New Bruswick, New Jersey: Rutgers University Press, 1958.

Because most scholars lack any basic faith, and have no regard for Christian values and meanings but are rather relativists, their learned works are too often "much ado about nothing." Libraries are often loaded with such studies while lacking in important source materials.

Men cannot give a meaning to history that they themselves lack, nor can they honor a past which indicts them for their present failures. It is no wonder then that, despite technical competence, American historians today are too often spiritual failures. Both the meaning of American history, and the spiritual and documentary resources, are generally by-passed.

A few illustrations of the contemporary philosophy as it approaches the American scene can be cited. An economist at a state college declared, in speaking on American economic history, that a major advance in history, and a realization of America's potentiality, came with the realization that the idea of an absolute law is invalid. This means, for example, that the gold standard is no longer needed, and that man writes his own laws in total relation to his needs, the only conceivable law being a relative one. This scholar's opinion is, of course, that which Eve listened to in Eden: every man his own god and law-maker, "knowing" which in Hebrew has the force of determining, his own laws as to what constitutes good and evil.

A second illustration: At Stanford, August 8, 1962, Eric F. Goldman, Princeton professor of history, defined greatness and near-greatness as submission to the popular will, to "the inevitable flow of feeling":

Truman and Eisenhower, Goldman said, will be remembered as "near great" presidents, not because of anything they particularly did, but because they finally, both after "conservative" starts, had "sense enough to not stand in

the way of the inevitable flow of feeling in the country." [11]
If such thinking is accepted, why not call Hitler great also
for having met "the inevitable flow of feeling" in Germany?
How can *any* popular regime be criticized?

A third illustration, from an influential government serv-
ant in the New Deal era, Francis Biddle, in a widely praised
book:

> All his life Holmes held to the survival of the strong, and
> did not disguise his view that the Sherman Act was a
> humbug, based on economic ignorance and incompetence,
> and that the Interstate Commerce Commission was not a
> fit body to be entrusted with rate making. However, as
> he said to Pollock, he was so skeptical about our knowl-
> edge of goodness or badness of laws that he had no prac-
> tical criticism except what the crowd wants. Personally
> he would bet that the crowd if it knew more wouldn't
> want what it does.
>
> In my brief life of Justice Holmes I commented on certain
> of his economic theories: and John W. Davis, who was
> Solicitor General of the United States from 1913 to 1918,
> when he read it, wrote to me that, after argument in an
> antitrust case, he walked away from the Court with the
> Justice. "Mr. Soliciter," asked Holmes, "how many more
> of the economic policy cases have you got?" "Quite a
> basketful," Davis answered. "Well," said the Justice,
> "Bring 'em on and we'll decide 'em. Of course I know, and
> every other sensible man knows, that the Sherman law is
> damned nonsense, but if my country wants to go to hell,
> I am here to help it." [12]

To the objection that "this course was Hitler's test," i.e.,
Holmes' belief *that truth was the majority vote of that
country that could lick all others*," Biddle could offer no

[11] Dan Schwartz, "WWII Changes Feelings About Policies: Goldman," in *Stanford Summer Weekly*, Stanford, California, vol. 8,
no. 7, August 9, 1962, p. 1.

[12] Francis Biddle: *Justice Holmes, Natural Law, and the Supreme
Court*, p. 8f. The Oliver Wendell Holmes Devise Lectures, 1960.
New York: Macmillan, 1961.

real answer.[13] There is no essential difference between Holmes' point of view and that of the savages of New Guinea studied recently by the Harvard-Peabody Expedition of 1961. For these people, rape, for example, is cited as fully right: "It is not a question of Weaklekek's lending support to a man (the rapist) who is in the wrong, for Asukwan is not really in the wrong. Asukwan took Palek's wife because his strength gave him that right; the only wrong involved is Palek's weakness."[14] When the doctrine of the supreme court and of historians begins to find common ground with that of savages, our own decline into barbarism is not far from sight.

This relativism not only prevails in politics, courts, and historiography, but also in most seminaries and churches. It is held, explicitly or implicitly, that Satan's theory is sound, namely that autonomous man is his own god and law-maker. The only god such men will recognize is one who abdicates in favor of man or is a limited god who is not truly in control. The issue is thus ultimately a religious one: on the one hand, the anarchy of autonomous man, whose only hope is then in majority law and hence collectivism since he has no law but man's law, or else the absolute and sovereign God and His unchanging law. The second faith leads to constitutionalism, a belief in fundamental law, and to action as well as historiography in terms of that faith. Relativism leads to tyranny and chaos, to moral and social decay. The issue man faces in historiography is basically the same one which confronts him in every area of life: the religious issue.

One more related issue needs to be noted. In 1782, Christopher Gadsen wrote to Francis Marion, reflecting a common opinion, "For it is essential to a Republic to have its

[13] *Ibid.*, p. 46f.
[14] Peter Matthiessen: *Under the Mountain Wall*, A Chronicle of two seasons in the Stone Age, p. 227. New York: Viking Press, 1962.

Laws plain and simple, as far as possible, and known to every member of the least attention." [15] Constitutional language, as well as early American law generally, was written in terms of this faith. The law now, however, is deliberately a specialist's function, and the increasing contempt for juries is a part of this same hostility to lay participation in the world of law. This is more than a development in expertise: it is an expression of a philosophy which finds voice in historiography as well. Bancroft, Hildreth, Prescott, and Motley were as careful researchers as any scholars today, and their works often more learned as well as longer. But they wrote with the general public in mind and were received by it: "historians had not yet begun to write largely for one another." [16] Because their philosophies, however transitional, still utilized the common background of faith in fundamental law, they saw the function of history-writing not in terms of technical shop talk within a limited profession but as an essential aspect of man's self-understanding and an instrument to his destiny, and their readers saw history as important to themselves in these terms. The historian is too often engaged today in a fallacious quest for anonymity behind a facade of "scientific" and "objective" scholarship which fails to hide either his relativism or his prejudices, and, once relativism is adopted, the writer's predilections become only prejudices. Philosophy today is too often left to the Marxist historian, whose "scientific" history is hostile to relativism and hence intensely concerned with communication with the masses. The breakdown of the religious and philosophical presuppositions of culture is followed by a decline in communication between segments of the population. Many historians today are as contemptuous of any attempt at general communication as

[15] Robert Allen Rutland: *The Birth of the Bill of Rights, 1776-1791*, p. 79. Chapel Hill: University of North Carolina Press, 1955.
[16] Michael Kraus: *A History of American History*, p. 183. New York: Farrar and Rinehart, 1937.

they are of meaning in history. However much they may deny it, their contempt of history is as real as that of Bismarck or Ford. The restoration of communication is dependent upon the basically religious issue of historiography.

APPENDIX 2

THE HERESY OF THE FAITHFUL

Many people excuse the extensive apostasy in the Church by pointing to original sin. Man is so great a sinner, we are told, that we should not be surprised at the extensive sway of unbelief in the very hearts of the faithful, let alone the world. We are reminded that the heart of man "is deceitful above all things, and desperately wicked: who can know it?" (Jer. 19:9). This is true, but the Scripture is not a Manichaean document. It does not assert that Satan and sin have a power equal to or greater than God and His grace. On the contrary, "God is greater than our hearts" (I John 3:20), and "greater is he that is in you, than he that is in the world" (I John 4:4). Great and almighty is our sovereign and triune God, and we cannot limit His power without sinning, nor can we ascribe the helplessness of the church to the greater power of sin and Satan. Rather, we must ascribe it to the heresy and laziness of believers, who limit God in their unbelief.

Related to this acceptance of apostasy, which is an implicit acceptance of the superiority of Satan, is the surrender of this world to Satan and to unbelievers. The whole of the Old Testament speaks of God's judgment against all ungodly nations, and St. Paul speaks in Hebrews 12:18-29 of the second shaking, the judgment of men and nations in the Gospel age, so that the things which cannot be shaken may alone remain. Christ who arose from the dead in the same body in which He was crucified set forth by His resurrection His victory over history as well as in eternity, over matter as well as in spirit. The work of God's judgments in history is to clear the way for Christ's Kingdom to prevail, heralded in Revelation 11:15 with the glorious proclamation, "The kingdoms of this world are become the kingdoms of our Lord and of his Christ; and he shall reign for ever and ever."

Can we surrender the world to Satan and be true to Scripture? One fine pastor has said that all "matters of political, economic and social concern" should be by-passed by the clergy:

> When you remember what Jesus said about the superiority of the wisdom of the "children of this generation" to that of the "children of light" in such matters (Luke 16:8), you know that society can manage its affairs quite well without the benefit of the clergy.

Let us call this interpretation what it is: *blasphemy!* Is the world better off if the clergy fail to proclaim and apply the Word of God to all things? And what did our Lord teach in Luke 16:8? Did He ask us to yield the world to the "children of this generation," or did He urge us to apply our wisdom even more earnestly? R. C. H. Lenski, in *The Interpretation of St. Luke's Gospel* (p. 830), summarizes the meaning:

> Thus: the *fully developed unrighteousness* we see in this man as regards the unrighteous mammon is to help us to see and to inspire us to attain the complete contrary, *the fully developed righteousness* with which we are to handle this unrighteous mammon: first, in the use to which we put it (v. 9); second, in the estimate we put upon it, which underlies any use we make of it (v. 10-12); third, in the resistance which we offer it, this underlying both the use and the estimate (v. 13).

Unbelief does *not* give superior wisdom, nor does regeneration make men idiots in the affairs of the world, that we should turn the management of society over to unbelievers! Rather, no man is better able to manage himself *and* the affairs of the world than the instructed Christian, and it is the duty of the clergy to instruct the believers in all things according to the infallible Word of God.

Some men claim the authority of Luther for this retreat from the world, this Protestant version of monastic withdrawal. Instead, its origin is in Pietism, which returned the medieval spirit to the church and withdrew it from the world. Instead of a Reformation concern with the whole counsel of God, Pietism concerned itself only with the soul and surrendered the world to the devil. With Pietism, Protestantism ceased to be the army of God, going forth to conquer in Christ's name, and the church became instead a kind of new monastary, where men could retreat from the world and its problems and contemplate heaven.

This writer received a letter from a fine and faithful pastor, criticizing him for speaking on economics in a church building, in the parish hall. Preaching on the Gospel, the doctrine of justification, he defined as preaching on "absolutes," and all other teaching dealt with things relative. But the whole word of God is true, and the Scripture speaks to the *whole* of man's life!

The following is my answer to the letter, reprinted on request, because so many Christians are disturbed by the limitations in their clergy's preaching due to Pietism:

Dear Pastor —:

Your gracious letter arrived today, and I hasten to answer it before it gets lost in a hundred or more letters which have accumulated during my travels.

We are agreed, I am sure from your letter, in affirming the infallibility of Scripture, justification by faith, and the sovereignty of the triune God. We alike hold to the doctrine of creation and the fall, and the depravity of man. The difference is, I think, practically summed up in your suggestion,

"According to our understanding, (a common one, I believe), a public minister of the Gospel is representative of Christ, and therefore under a restriction to declare the whole counsel *of God*.

"For that reason I think that you would be in a more effective position if you were to lecture on such a subject as economics as a lay specialist rather than an ordained minister of the Orthodox Presbyterian Church. Perhaps it would even be helpful to use a public auditorium rather than a church building—simply because of identification."

At this point, I would disagree, and I believe, from my reading, that I would have Luther on my side.

There are two approaches to subjects, a humanistic one, of which there are many variations, and a theocentric and Biblical one. My recent lecture in Sunnyvale on economics, the third of a series on money, of which the first dealt with the exegetical foundations, has a theocentric and Biblical basis, and my assertion was that the world, and economics, is under God's law, NOT under man-made law.

For me to declare the whole counsel of God means exactly that. The law of God deals extensively with economics, i.e., with money, lending, usury, agriculture, business, etc. (I am enclosing some copies of my recent newsletters, of which Number 8 deals with certain aspects of economics relating to debt. These I dealt with in an earlier talk at Sunnyvale.). One brilliant economist, who has studied the Old Testament and New Testament laws and references to money, has pointed out that fractional reserve banking is clearly prohibited by Biblical law, although, of course, modern banking terminology is not used.

I take the law of God very seriously. I believe that man is saved from the law as a handwriting of ordinances against him, so that man is no longer, as a Christian, under the law as an indictment, but he is under the law as a way of life. The law is now written on the tables of his heart (the sign of the new covenant), and is his joy to keep. Man is not saved to have other gods, commit adultery, kill, steal, or covet, or to break any of God's laws, but, having now a new nature, delights in God's will to the extent that he is sanctified.

The ceremonial and sacrificial law is clearly fulfilled in Christ's atoning death and resurrection. Certain other laws have been subjected to changes by apostolic teaching, or our Lord's teaching, as witness the penalty for adultery to divorce, and the revision of the day of worship, and the end of the old Sabbath regulations (Col. 2:16f., etc.). Certainly the Reformers did not treat the Old Testament laws lightly, as witness their concern with usury.

I believe that it is a part of our modern apostasy that we have abandoned much of the world to the devil and restricted the Gospel to a narrow realm. The doctrine of creation is to me the cornerstone of our faith. Because the Holy Trinity created all things, all things are understandable only in terms of the triune God, and only He can redeem His creation. Moreover, only under His law can the creation function without ruin. Therefore, God's word must be declared for every realm: we must have a Christian economics, philosophy (which begins with the premise of the infallible word and the triune God), historiography, literature, law, political science, and so on.

I wrote *The Messianic Character of American Education* as a carefully documented statement of my thesis, that education apart from Christian theistic principles is destructive of itself and of man. I believe that the same is true of every other field of study.

The doctrine of the bodily resurrection of our Lord is in part a declaration that God's salvation is not restricted to the soul alone, but that time and history as well as eternity, the body as well as the soul, are destined to share in the glorious salvation of our God.

I would agree that the *church* has no jurisdiction apart from the word of God, the sacraments, and the administration of godly discipline within the church. But the

143

word of God speaks to every condition and to every realm of life.

My point, in dealing with economics, was, in all three talks, Biblical. I dealt with the Biblical laws concerning money and debt in the first two, and, in the third, I simply emphasized the fact that it is God's law that governs the universe, not the man-made power ploys of contemporary politicians. I was giving a lecture rather than a sermon, but, had I been preaching, I would simply have been exegetical. And debased money is clearly condemned in Scripture, as witness Isaiah's indictment (1:22, which clearly refers to the debasing of silver and the adulterating of wine).

One of the fearful conditions of our days is that, apart from the modernistic, humanistic, and apostate schemes offered to men today, there is little to be heard except secular conservatism, which is in essence simply another form of humanism and equally to be condemned. I believe in the necessity for Christian conservatism, and I believe that we shall be under God's judgment if we neglect to proclaim the whole counsel of God for every realm, church, state, school, philosophy (where the great classic is Luther's *Bondage of the Will*), economics, political science, etc. This is not making Christ partisan: it is simply asserting, to use the old Reformation battle cry, "The Crown Rights of King Jesus" over every realm.

I write this, not in any sense in criticism of your position, but in the prayerful hope that you will recognize the full-orbed claims of our Redeemer.

Very sincerely,
R. J. Rushdoony

INDEX

145

146

Rutland, R. A., 138n
Rymer, Thomas, 77

Saint Thomas' School, 39n
Satan, 139f.
Saturnalia, 118
Search for historical Jesus, 1
Schilder, K., 26f.
Schlosser, W. E., 95
Schoeck, H., 126
Schwartz, Don, 136n
Schweitzer, A., 57
Scriven, M., 97n
Shafer, B. C., 125n
Socialism, 7, 47ff., 77f., 80, 83-86
Social Science, 19
Soule, L. C., 35n
Spear, Percival, 37n
Spitz, L. W., 97n
Stalin, 54
Stalingrad, 1
Stampp, K. M., 112, 114
Stowe, D. M., 92n
Swedenborg, 133f.

Tennyson, A., 113
Tibet, 58f.
Time, 3f., 10ff., 22, 28-39, 58-62
Tocqueville, Alexis de, 36
Tolerance, 55, 57
Torrance, T. F., 43f.
Tradition, 73, 90f.
Tree of Life, 116f., 124
Trinity, Doctrine of, 24
Truth, 10, 49, 63-73
Tyng, Stephen H., 16n

U.C.L.A., 97
Ultimate Decree, see Predestination
United Nations, 56, 115
U.S. News & World Report, 94n, 124n
Utopianism, 41, 60

Van Riessen, H., 41n
Van Til, Cornelius, 12, 14, 17n, 51, 52, 64, 69n, 126
Vindiciae Contra Tyrannos, 130
Virgin Birth, 105-110
Vision of God, 32
Voegelin, Eric, 64
Von Fersen, S., 53

Walker, Robert H., 130
Ward, Barbara, 123n
Watson, J. S., 100n
Weather modification, 123
Weaver, R. M., 64
Weisberger, B. A., 130n
Wenger, Joyce, 93n
Wescott, B. B., 40, 42
Westminster Confession of Faith, 17n, 57
Wiggins, James W., 126
Witherspoon, John, 128f.
Wood, Nathan R., 11n
Woodhouse, A. S. P., 36n
World Council of Churches, 90f.

Yale, 28